Bibliotherapy

Special Aspects of Education

A series of books edited by Roy Evans, Roehampton Institute of Higher Education, London, UK

This book is part of a series. The publisher will accept continuation orders which may be cancelled at any time and which provide for automatic billing and shipping of each title in the series upon publication. Please write for details.

Bibliotherapy
A Clinical Approach for Helping Children

JOHN T. PARDECK

Southwest Missouri State University, Springfield, USA

and

JEAN A. PARDECK

Blue Hills Homes Corporation, Missouri, USA

GORDON AND BREACH SCIENCE PUBLISHERS

Switzerland • Australia • Belgium • France • Germany • Great Britain •
India • Japan • Malaysia • Netherlands • Russia • Singapore • USA

First published 1993
Second printing 1994

Gordon and Breach Science Publishers S.A.
Y-Parc
Chemin de la Sallaz
1400 Yverdon, Switzerland

Library of Congress Cataloging-in-Publication Data

Bibliotherapy : a clinical approach for helping children / edited by
  John T. Pardeck and Jean A. Pardeck.
        p.   cm. -- (Special aspects of education ; v. 16)
  Includes bibliographical references and indexes.
  ISBN 3-7186-5347-8
  1. Bibliotherapy for children.   I. Pardeck, John T.   II. Pardeck,
Jean A.   III. Series.
  [DNLM: 1. Bibliotherapy--infancy & childhood.   W1 SP286 v. 16 /
WM 450.5.B5 B5812]
RJ505.B5B5   1993
618.92'89166--dc20
DNLM/DLC
for Library of Congress   93-49528
                                                                  CIP

To Jamie and Jonathan,
our preadolescents

Contents

Introduction to the Series

Increasingly in the last 10 to 15 years the published literature within the field of care education has become more specialised and focussed: an inevitable consequence of the information explosion and the wider scope of theoretical and practical knowledge being required of students in both the traditional and developing areas of professional training. Students within initial and post-initial training evidently need to have ready access to specialised theoretical and pedagogical resources relevant to the context of their future professional involvements which also develop special aspects of an area of study in a critically evaluative way.

In the study of education and pedagogy, the analytical and experimental approaches of psychology, philosophy, sociology, social anthropology, etc., have provided insights into teaching and learning, into schooling and education. Historically these disciplines have focussed their attention on relatively homogeneous populations. Increased worldwide mobility has created a need for a more pluralistic approach to education — particularly in Western countries — and a more broadly based concern for educational issues related in particular contexts. Hence, further literature has developed in recent years which is concerned with the pedagogical and curricular issues raised, for example, in connection with the "urban school", minority ethnic groups, disadvantaged and handicapped groups, and children who live apart from their families.

What is frequently missing from discipline-oriented studies is a real appreciation of context beyond the "general". What is often not present in the contextual study is an interdisciplinary analysis of the issue that provides a framework for practice.

The present series — "Special Aspects of Education" — is intended to bridge the gap between the problems of practice, as perceived in a variety of contexts, and theory, as derived from a variety of disciplines. Books accepted or commissioned for inclusion in the series will manifestly be expected to acknowledge the interdisciplinary nature of the issues and problems in the field of education and care and, addressing themselves to particular contexts, to provide a conceptual framework for identifying and meeting special educational needs.

Roy Evans

Preface

The purpose of this book is to provide professionals in the field of mental health with readily available information on literature that can effectively be used with clinical problems of children. The materials included in the work can also be used by those not necessarily trained in the area of mental health, but who, none the less, deal with children; this group includes parents, teachers, and librarians.

The clinical approach offered in the work is bibliotherapy. Bibliotherapy is an emerging clinical technique that is useful for working with children. Chapter 1 offers a detailed overview of the bibliotherapeutic approach, who uses it in practice, and a detailed review of the research on the topic of bibliotherapy.

Chapter 2 discusses the clinical applications of bibliotherapy. This chapter covers the principles of bibliotherapy, how one can use the approach in treatment, and clinical examples that include divorce and child abuse.

The clinical topics covered in the work focus on changing role models, the blended family, separation and divorce, child abuse, foster care, adoption, and childhood fears. There are over 350 annotated children's books presented in the work that deal with these clinical problems. The titles included are from the United Kingdom and the United States. A directory is offered that lists the addresses of publishers of the children's books found in the work.

Coverage and Scope

The books annotated in this work were mostly published in the 1980s; a limited number of children's books are included from other decades. The general criteria used for a book to be included were:

1. The book had to be a children's literary work that related to one or more of the clinical topics covered in the work.
2. The book had to have a child character or an animal character with human characteristics.

The work does not offer a literary review of the children's books included. What was used, however, was a more important clinical consideration, that being whether the literary work realistically dealt with one or more of the clinical problems covered in the work. Every effort was made to include children's books that accurately depict the clinical problems of concern.

Entries

The annotated entries included are arranged in alphabetical order by the author's last name. Many of the annotated literary works focus on more than one childhood clinical problem. However, the primary clinical problem covered in a given literary work determined the chapter under which it is included. For example, a book on child abuse may include some content on foster care. If the primary focus is on abuse, however, the book was placed in the chapter on child abuse. The annotated entries include an interest level (IL). The interest levels range from two to eighteen years of age.

Indexes

The author index is a guide to the individuals who wrote the books annotated in each chapter. The title index helps the reader locate a particular title. The numbers following the authors and titles in these two indexes refer to the page number where the entry can be found. A subject index allows the reader to refer to specific subjects covered in the annotated entries. Like the two other indexes, the subject index refers the reader to the appropriate page number within the book.

Acknowledgements

The authors would like to thank Emy Glass for typing the early drafts of the manuscript. Special thanks goes to Terry L. Brown for her excellent editing of the book. The authors also appreciate the encouragement of Lois Musick, Burl Musick, Ruth Russo, and Chic Russo.

Chapter 1

An Overview of Bibliotherapy

Books for centuries have worked as silent therapists for untold numbers. Through books readers can completely escape into new roles; they can vicariously sample lives and life–styles. Good fiction can provide clients with models to help them deal with presenting problems. Quality nonfiction, in particular self–help books, can provide clients with concrete suggestions and advice to help them deal with presenting problems.

The technique of using books in treatment is defined as bibliotherapy. Bibliotherapy has been known by many names, such as bibliocounseling, biblioeducation, bibliopsychology, library therapeutics, biblioprophylaxis, tutorial group therapy, and literatherapy (Rubin, 1978). Webster (1981) defines bibliotherapy as "guidance in the solution of personal problems through directed reading." Berry (1978) defines bibliotherapy as a family of techniques for structuring an interaction between a facilitator and a participant...based on their mutual sharing of literature. Over the last several years bibliotherapy has been used by a variety of helping professionals including counselors, psychologists, psychiatrists, and educators. Only recently have social workers begun to use bibliotherapy in clinical practice (Pardeck & Pardeck, 1987). The newly published *Dictionary of Social Work* by Barker (1987) does, however, include a comprehensive definition of bibliotherapy:

> The use of literature and poetry in the treatment of people with emotional problems or mental illness. Bibliotherapy is often used in social group work and group therapy and is reported to be effective with people of all ages, with people in institutions as well as outpatients, and with healthy people who wish to share literature as a means of personal growth and development. (p. 15)

Rubin (1978) notes that most professionals using bibliotherapy in practice have minimal preparation for using this intriguing technique. Pardeck and Pardeck (1987) conclude that social workers are the least likely to use bibliotherapy in practice, and few have formal clinical training in using books in social treatment.

Baruth and Burggraf (1984), Griffin (1984), and Pardeck and Pardeck (1984) all suggest that the major goals of bibliotherapy are as follows: (a) to provide information about problems, (b) to provide insight into problems, (c) to stimulate discussion about problems, (d) to communicate new values and attitudes, (e) to create an awareness that others have dealt with similar problems, and (f) to provide solutions to problems.

Much information can be conveyed through assigned and shared reading. Bibliotherapy allows one to learn new facts, different ways of approaching problems, and alternative ways of thinking about problems (Griffin, 1984). Since most clients have limited prior knowledge or personal experience with a presenting problem, bibliotherapy can provide useful insight into helping clients deal with problems.

Self–understanding and insight is an important goal of bibliotherapy (Baruth & Burggraf, 1984; Zaccaria & Moses, 1968). When therapists use fiction in bibliotherapy, clients read about a character facing a problem similar to their own; they may then identify with the character and in so doing gain awareness and understanding of their own motivation, feelings, and thoughts (Griffin, 1984). By reading about a story character's conflicts, cognition, and emotional reactions, clients gain insight into a problem situation (Pardeck & Pardeck, 1983).

Bibliotherapy is an excellent technique for stimulating discussion about a problem which may not otherwise be discussed because of fear, guilt, or shame (McKinney, 1977). Reading about a character in fiction who has dealt with a problem similar to his or her own may help the client verbalize feelings about the problem to the clinician.

Bibliotherapy can help clients confront and change presenting problems as they read about others who have done so successfully. The physically disabled person, for example, can read about a character who has successfully dealt with a disability. The disabled individual may learn that many others have faced the same problem, had similar feelings of inadequacy and failure, and yet found a way to succeed to some degree and develop self–realization about the disability (Pardeck & Pardeck, 1984).

History of Bibliotherapy

Books have been used as a resource for helping people cope for centuries. In ancient Thebes, for example, a library entry was inscribed "The Healing Place of the Soul." The ancient Thebans cherished books for their value as a source for improving the quality of life. Schrank and Engels (1981) have pointed out that the practice of bibliotherapy can be traced back to Thebes and since then has been used as a helping resource for instruction and healing.

Several early American schoolbooks such as the *New England Primer* and the *McGuffy Readers* were used with the intent not only of teaching children how to read but also for helping them to develop character and positive values, and to improve personal adjustment (Spache, 1974). Present educators, including many clinicians, have come to realize that books can play a positive role in helping people deal with personal adjustment problems, including the problems of everyday life.

Bibliotherapy as a recognized treatment approach really evolved only quite recently. This development is roughly dated as occurring around the turn of the 20th century. Two early advocates of bibliotherapy in the 20th century were Doctors Karl and William Menninger. Numerous articles appeared in the professional literature in the 1940s; these often focused on the psychological validity of this emerging treatment technique (Bernstein, 1983). During the 1950s some of the seminal thinking on the subject of bibliotherapy was done by Shrodes (1949), who examined the state of the art, thus

influencing the field tremendously from a philosophical view. Shrodes'
(1949) early definition of bibliotherapy "as a process of dynamic interaction
between the personality of the reader and literature under the guidance of a
trained helper" continues to heavily influence the field today (p. 22).
Recently, Pardeck and Pardeck (1989) have argued that bibliotherapy does
not have to be a process necessarily guided by a trained therapist. As
pointed out later in this book, bibliotherapy can be implemented by individuals not trained as therapists. For example, a parent or teacher can successfully use bibliotherapy to help children cope with problems related to development and personal adjustment.

In the 1960s, Hannigan and Henderson (1963) conducted extensive on
site research regarding the impact of bibliotherapy on young drug abusers
close to parole. Their research comprises some of the early efforts to test the
effectiveness of bibliotherapy as a treatment tool. Since the 1960s, numerous studies have been conducted on the effectiveness of bibliotherapy in
helping people deal with emotional and adjustment problems. Even though
bibliotherapy has been found to be an effective clinical tool, critics of bibliotherapy continue to be very vocal (Craighead, McNamara, & Horan, 1984).

Who Uses Bibliotherapy

Pardeck and Pardeck (1987) report that among helping professionals, social
workers are the least likely to use bibliotherapy. They found in a content
analysis of articles published from 1980 to 1983 in *Social Casework* and
Social Work that only seven articles on bibliotherapy appeared in these two
journals. In turn, *School Counselor* and *Elementary School Guidance and
Counseling* published over 40 articles on bibliotherapy during the same time
period. Pardeck and Pardeck (1987) thus concluded that school counselors
are probably well acquainted with bibliotherapy, as reflected through the
works published in two core counseling journals. Social workers have little
access to information on bibliotherapy because little is written about the approach in professional social work journals.

Additional studies have surveyed practitioners in other fields and found
that bibliotherapy is widely used by counselors, psychologists, psychiatrists, and medical doctors. Atwater and Smith (1987) found heavy use of
bibliotherapy among counselors. Smith and Burkhalter (1987) report that
the more experienced the therapist, the more likely he or she is to use bibliotherapy in practice. Starker (1986) reports that among 487 practitioners surveyed in a large metropolitan area within the United States, 88% of psychologists, 59% of psychiatrists, and 88% of medical doctors responding
used bibliotherapy in their practice. Starker (1988) in a national study found
that almost 60% of psychologists used bibliotherapy in practice occasionally
and 24% used it often.

In sum, bibliotherapy is a popular treatment technique among certain
helping professionals, including counselors, psychologists, and psychiatrists. Social workers appear less likely to use the bibliotherapeutic technique.

Research on Bibliotherapy

Both fiction and nonfiction can be used when treating clients with biblio-therapy. Even though some recent evidence suggests fiction can be used as a powerful therapeutic tool, the research clearly concludes that behaviorally oriented reading materials in the form of self–help books have the greatest empirical support as successful clinical tools.

Prior to the 1980s, numerous studies were conducted on using fiction as a therapeutic tool. The research falls into roughly the following categories: academic achievement, assertiveness, attitude change, behavioral change, marital relations, reducing fear, self–concept improvement, and therapeutic effectiveness.

Academic Achievement

Most of the studies suggest that bibliotherapy does not increase academic achievement; however, a few do report that it can impact academic achieve-ment positively. Whipple (1978) concluded that bibliotherapy was able to raise academic achievement in the biological sciences of students in a state reformatory. King (1972) found that underachieving children who received bibliotherapy in addition to regular language arts classes showed significant gains over the underachieving students who attended only language arts classes. A study by Lundstein (1972) reported that bibliotherapy helped in-crease communication skills of elementary school students.

Other researchers have found that bibliotherapy did not affect academic achievement positively. Bigge and Sandefur (1960) discovered it did not help high school students to improve their academic achievement. Dixon (1974) concluded that bibliotherapy in conjunction with remedial reading instruction did not increase reading skills. Livengood (1961) also reported that bibliotherapy failed to increase the reading skills of students. A study by Ponder (1968) found that bibliotherapy did not increase academic achievement in a group of poverty level students. Research conducted by Schultheis (1969) found that fifth-and sixth-grade students did not gain in reading achievement after going through a bibliotherapy experience.

Assertiveness

Research suggests that bibliotherapy can increase assertiveness levels. McGovern (1976) reported that bibliotherapy increased assertiveness in subjects subsequent to assertiveness training over those who did not experi-ence bibliotherapy. Allen (1978) and Nesbitt (1977) found that assertive be-haviors increased as subjects completed a bibliotherapy program.

Attitude Change

Bibliotherapy has been found to change attitudes. Jackson (1944), Litcher and Johnson (1969), and Standley and Standley (1970) reported that bibliotherapy positively changed attitudes of majority group members toward blacks. Smith (1948) concluded that students could report ways that bibliotherapy changed their attitudes. Tatara (1964) found bibliotherapy successful in changing attitudes toward scientists. Wilson (1951) reported positive effects of bibliotherapy toward changing severe attitudinal problems.

Behavioral Change

The findings suggest that bibliotherapy can change behaviors of individuals. A research project by Lewis (1967) concluded that when children took part in a bibliotherapy program, the children increased expression of aggressive behaviors but did not decrease selfish behaviors. Shirley (1966) found that students were able to report how books changed their behaviors. A study by McClasky (1966) reported that bibliotherapy positively changed behaviors in emotionally disturbed clients.

Marital Relations

Most of the research suggests that bibliotherapy does not improve marital relationships. Carr (1975) found that bibliotherapy was not useful as an approach for helping people deal with marital conflict. Barton (1977) also concluded that bibliotherapy did not help couples solve marital problems. A study by Baum (1977) reported that using bibliotherapy in groups for marital enrichment did not significantly differ from using a more typical and structured format with groups.

Reducing Fear

Initial research suggested bibliotherapy had little effect on reducing fear. Even though Webster (1961) found bibliotherapy did reduce fears in first graders, studies by Dixon (1974) and Link (1977) did not find bibliotherapy effective in reducing fear and anxiety in individuals they studied. However, recent research by Chambers (1985), Dixon (1988), Mackenzie (1989), Tindall (1986), Tremewan and Strongman (1991), and Tucker (1981) concluded that fiction provides children with an effective means for dealing with fears.

Self–Concept and Self–Development

The research presents a mixed picture of the impact of bibliotherapy on self–concept and self–development. Kanaan (1975), King (1972), and Penna (1975) reported that bibliotherapy had a positive impact on the self–concepts of children. Studies by Caffee (1975), Dixon (1974), Roach (1975), and Shearon (1975), however, did not show bibliotherapy to improve the self–concepts of subjects participating in their research.

A number of studies concluded that bibliotherapy can positively impact self–development. Appleberry (1969) found bibliotherapy useful for improving mental health in a nonclinical population of grade school children. Bibliotherapy helped college students improve problem solving, develop insight, and resolve stress (Amato, 1957). Mattera (1961) found that reading books helped children in their problem solving. Finally, a study by Herminghaus (1954) reported that bibliotherapy helped to produce desirable personal behaviors among a group of children participating in his research. Studies not finding bibliotherapy useful for self–development include research by Bigge and Sandefur (1960), who reported that bibliotherapy did not improve self–development in a nonclinical population of high school students. Stephens (1974) concluded that bibliotherapy did not increase self–reliance in grade school students.

Therapeutic Usefulness

Most studies conducted on bibliotherapy suggest that it can be a valuable therapeutic technique. Whipple (1978) found that bibliotherapy helped to improve the mental health of inmates. Muehleisen (1976) revealed that bibliotherapy reduced psychiatric symptoms and improved ego strengths in clients. Saper (1967) reported that bibliotherapy in combination with group therapy created greater involvement, problem solving behaviors, and insight in subjects than group therapy alone.

The research conducted prior to the 1980s suggests that bibliotherapy is an effective tool for increasing assertiveness, changing attitudes, changing behaviors, enhancing self–development, and as a therapeutic technique. The effectiveness of bibliotherapy for increasing academic achievement, improving marital relations, reducing fears, and changing self–concept is not strongly supported in the research literature. Many of these studies prior to the 1980s do conclude, though, that bibliotherapy is a useful tool for helping children cope with problems.

During the 1980s, 14 research projects were conducted on the effectiveness of bibliotherapy as a resource for changing behavior through self–help books. Of these studies, only three report negative findings concerning the effectiveness of the bibliotherapeutic technique. Four studies report that bibliotherapy can change inappropriate behavior of adolescents (Frankel & Merbaun, 1982; Harbaugh, 1984; Miller, 1982; and Swantic, 1986). Pezzot–Pearce, LeBow, and Pearce (1982) concluded that the reading of a behavioral manual alone had a positive effect on clients' losing weight. Rucker (1983) and Cuevas (1984) found a behaviorally based self–help approach effective in treating chronic headaches and obesity. Bailey (1982) concluded that reading a self–help manual had a positive effect on treating insomnia. Of three studies using comparison treatment groups, one found self–help books useful in changing children's behavior (Klingman, 1985), another found books useful for improving conversation skills (Black, 1981), and a third found them effective in weight loss (Black & Threlfall, 1986). Yet a study by Conner (1981) reported that self–help books did not improve interpersonal skills, and Galliford (1982) concluded that self–help books were not effective in reducing weight. Giles (1986) reported that reading stories describing reinforcement contingencies did not shape the immediate behavior of clinically disturbed children. However, the majority of studies conducted during the 1980s suggest that behaviorally based reading programs in the form of self–help reading materials are effective in positively impacting clinical problems.

The research conducted during the 1980s suggests that poetry, fiction, and inspirational readings have been found less effective than self–help books. This may be the case because behaviorally oriented self–help readings are more amenable to empirical-based research than fiction.

During the 1980s, Bohlmann (1986), Ray (1983), and Taylor (1982) all found fiction to be a useful tool for improving self–concept. However, DeFrances, Dexter, Leary, and MacMullen (1982) and Shafron (1983) found no support for fiction as a resource for improving self–concept.

Other important studies reported mixed findings for the effectiveness of fiction in treating clinical problems. Ford, Bashford, and DeWitt (1984) reported some support for its effectiveness in marital counseling. Libman, Fichten, Brender, Burstein, Cohen, and Binik (1984) found fiction was not a useful resource for treating sexual dysfunction. However, Dodge, Glasgow, and O'Neill (1982) determined that fiction was useful for treating sexual dysfunction. Finally, Morris–Vann (1983) and Sadler (1982) concluded that fiction was effective in improving emotional adjustment of clients.

It is apparent that numerous studies have proven that bibliotherapy is a useful therapeutic tool; however, one should not overlook those studies suggesting it is not effective as a therapeutic medium. One should clearly note that the majority of the studies conducted in the 1980s support the effectiveness of using nonfiction as a resource in the bibliotherapy process.

Values of Bibliotherapy

Practitioners who work with clients experiencing problems see great value in bibliotherapy. In particular, bibliotherapy can help clients gain insight into problems, provide clients with techniques for relaxation and diversion, and help clients focus outside the self.

Even though one of the core criticisms of bibliotherapy has been that it is not an exact science, many practitioners have found it to be an effective treatment tool. What should be noted, however, is that virtually all of the helping therapies are far from exact; bibliotherapy is no exception. Bibliotherapy may be more complex than other therapies because one must be skilled both in selecting literature that parallels the problem facing a client and in knowing how to use such literature as a therapeutic medium (Pardeck, 1990). If one can combine these steps successfully, bibliotherapy can prove to be a very valuable treatment approach.

Bibliotherapy can also be useful for helping individuals enhance interpersonal relationships. For example, if a client is having problems with family or peer relationships, bibliotherapy can help the client develop tolerance and understanding of others and formulate a more objective approach to dealing with problems. After reading about how other families solve problems, an individual may come up with solutions to family problems. In turn, an individual having problems with peers can gain insight into the complexities of peer relationships through reading about other peer situations. This important insight into the problem can lead to the exploration of solutions with the help of the practitioner (Pardeck, 1990).

Bibliotherapy is a powerful tool for helping clients deal with physical or emotional disabilities. Through reading about a disability and gaining insight into how a book character copes with a similar problem, a client can develop solutions for dealing with the disability. Disabled people may even see improvement with their disability as they read about it in literature (Bernstein, 1983).

Finally, bibliotherapy may also be viewed as a preventive tool. For example, an acting out adolescent may gain insight through literature about his or her behavior and find solutions for preventing future problems. An individual can read about an emerging developmental crisis and formulate strategies for dealing with it. Adolescents often have great concern about human sexuality; literature can help children cope with problems and issues related to sexuality. Books can also help clients who are confronted with problems see that they are not alone, and that many others have solved or learned to live with similar problems.

Choosing Books

Coleman and Ganong (1988) identify a number of criteria that should be considered when selecting books for treatment. First, a book must match the client's reading ability. A book that is too difficult will not be read or will simply frustrate the client. A book that is too simple, in turn, may be insulting and thus damage the therapeutic relationship.

A second point to consider is the number of issues and problems presented in the book. Coleman and Ganong (1987) conclude that the more issues dealt with in a book, the better the quality of the book. Clients will be more apt to read a book that parallels their own life experiences.

A third factor is the quality and quantity of the advice presented. Ideally, a number of possible solutions should be offered. If such is the case for a given book, a client with the support of the helping person can come up with solutions to a presenting problem.

A fourth area to consider is how realistically the problem is depicted in the book. This point is extremely important when using fiction as a treatment resource. A well–balanced perspective in the book is very important. Realistic solutions for a problem should also be presented in the book.

A final consideration is the tone of the book. Coleman and Ganong (1987) suggest, for instance, that a book or books used in bibliotherapy should include the valuable quality of humor.

Rosen (1981) supplies a number of additional criteria therapists can use in choosing books for bibliotherapy, based on an empirical framework. These criteria are particularly useful for choosing self–help books for therapeutic intervention. Rosen suggests the following questions should be explored before using a book in treatment:

1. What claims exist in the title or contents of a book that define the text as a do–it–yourself treatment program?
2. Has the author attempted to convey accurate information regarding the empirical support for the self-help program?
3. Does the book provide a basis for self–diagnosis, and have the methods for self diagnosis been evaluated to establish rates of false positives and false negatives
4. Do the techniques in the book have empirical support?
5. Has the book been tested for its clinical efficacy, and under what conditions of usage have the tests been conducted?
6. In light of the above questions, what is the accuracy of any claims made in the title or content of the book?
7. Can comparisons be made between the book under review and other self–help books on the same topic?

Practitioners will have more confidence when they assign readings for treatment if they use the above criteria to assess the quality of a book. Obviously, it would be extremely difficult to identify books which meet all the above criteria (Rosen, 1987). The greater the number of the above criteria a book meets, the better the book is suited for bibliotherapy treatment.

Using Books in Treatment

The following sections describes the use of bibliotherapy through self–help and fiction books. The helping person who has a more cognitive–behavioral approach to practice is more apt to use self–help books, whereas fiction is more likely to be used by therapists with a psychodynamic orientation.

Self–Help Literature

Numerous self–help books have been developed over the last several years. Practitioners will find that self–help books can be an excellent adjunct to practice. Self–help books may be used as a technique for offering various options for the client to choose from in dealing with a problem. These options will provide different ways of thinking, coping, and acting when addressing a clinical problem. When problem solving options are offered through books, they can enhance the therapeutic process. The therapist may find that if a problem solving option is offered as part of the traditional therapeutic approach, the client may reject it; however, if the therapist has the client read about the option, the client may be more likely to consider it as a serious possibility for solving a problem. Coleman and Ganong (1988) conclude such a strategy of problem solving is particularly appropriate for adolescents.

Self–help books often contain structured activities that clients can participate in. These activities are designed to encourage problem solving, to stimulate communication between client and practitioner, or to help clients identify and process their feelings. Such activities can be assigned as homework in therapy or as part of group therapy, or can be used during individual-based therapy (Coleman & Ganong, 1988).

Self–help books can also be used to facilitate role-playing. Clients can role-play actions described in a book or they can demonstrate ways of responding to certain social situations. After reading a self–help book clients can brainstorm alternatives from what was read, such as other ways of dealing with the events portrayed in the book or character strengths not mentioned in the book (Coleman & Ganong, 1988).

Glasgow and Rosen (1978, 1979) offer a number of ways self–help books can be used in the treatment process:

The *Self-Administered* approach is a strategy in which the client receives written material from the helping person, has no contact with the practitioner beyond the initial session, and then ends with a post–test. This strategy is sometimes referred to as the "no–contact" self–help therapeutic orientation.

The *Minimal–Contact* self–help approach is a treatment strategy involving the practitioner providing written materials to the client; however, the therapeutic role is expanded to written correspondence, phone calls, and infrequent meetings with the client. An example of this approach includes the various weight–control self–help books which call for only minimal contact with the practitioner mainly through frequent follow–up calls.

Therapist–Administered self–help books are those which the client receives at the beginning of treatment. The therapist uses the self–help materials at each therapeutic session. During the therapy session the written materials are discussed, emphasizing the ways in which these materials can help the client solve the presenting problem.

The *Therapist–Direct* strategy refers to the traditional, weekly interview treatment approach in which contact with the therapist is the focus of intervention. The self–help materials are often used between therapy sessions in the form of homework assignments or other intervention activities. The treatment offered by the therapist during weekly sessions is often reinforced in the self–help manual. In some self–help manuals, self–monitoring forms are available which are designed to help the client to continue working on a problem between sessions.

Self–help reading materials can be grouped according to the conditions of intended usage. Often self–help manuals are written in a way that assumes it is possible for a person confronted with a problem to purchase reading materials over the counter and implement the self–help plan without the assistance of a practitioner. This approach is not endorsed by clinicians; however, for certain clients confronted with relatively minor problems, this form of self–help can be useful.

The more sound approach is to use the participant self–help manual. Such an approach demands that the therapist be involved in varying degrees in the therapeutic process. The participant self–help manual typically includes self-monitoring forms, descriptions of activities and exercises, and brief summaries of specific procedures. As with all approaches to bibliotherapy, the participant self–help approach is designed as an adjunct to therapy.

Fiction Books

Bibliotherapy can be implemented through fiction. When fiction is used in treatment, the fiction must accurately portray the problem confronting the client. After the client reads the fictional work, the practitioner helps the client develop insight and solutions to the problem through the literature.

The bibliotherapeutic approach when using fiction consists of three phases: *identification and projection, abreaction and catharsis, and insight and integration.* Identification and projection is the first stage of the process. During this stage, the client with the help of the practitioner begins to see similarities between his or her problem and a book character's problem. The practitioner's role during this initial stage is to help the client interpret the motives of the story character and provide insight into the relationships among various book characters. The practitioner during this stage helps the client make inferences regarding the meaning of the story and its application to the client's problem.

Once identification and projection have occurred, the therapist moves the client to the abreaction and catharsis stage. In order for catharsis to occur, the client must experience an emotional release that is expressed in a number of ways, including verbal and nonverbal means. The involvement of the therapist at this stage of intervention is critical and is unique to bibliotherapy versus the normal reading process. During the abreaction and catharsis stage, the practitioner must monitor details such as the client's reaction to the literature, the degree of similarity between the client's emotional experience and the problem being treated, and the emotional experiences of the client throughout the process of his or her identification with the story.

The final stage of bibliotherapy is insight and integration. During this stage, the client is guided by the practitioner to recognize solutions to a problem through the literature. During this stage the client develops new strategies for dealing with the presenting problem.

The stages of the bibliotherapy process correspond closely to the phases of Freudian psychotherapy, one of the theoretical bases upon which bibliotherapy is founded. Shrodes (1949, p. 22), a pioneer in the development of bibliotherapy, states:

Identification is generally defined as an adaptive mechanism which the human being utilizes, largely unconsciously, to augment his self–regard. It takes the form of a real or imagined affiliation of oneself with another person, a group of persons, or with some institution, or even with a symbol. There is usually involved admiration for the object of one's identification, a tendency to imitate, and a sense of loyalty and belongingness.

Projection has two common usages in the literature. It consists of the at-
tribution to others of one's own motives or emotions in order to ascribe
blame to another instead of to oneself. The term is also used to describe
one's perception, apperception, and cognition of the world and people.
Catharsis is used synonymously with abreaction to denote the uncen-
sored and spontaneous release of feelings: in the Aristotelian sense it
means the purging of emotional awareness of one's motivation, experiences, and subsequent abreaction.

As can be seen, when using fiction in bibliotherapy treatment, the orientation is psychodynamic. When practitioners use self–help books, they have a
tendency to lean toward the cognitive–behavioral orientation (Pardeck,
1990). One should note two important points: (a) fiction, like self–help
books, is seen as an adjunct to the total treatment process; and (b) the research evidence suggests that there is greater support for behaviorally oriented self–help books versus the use of fiction in treatment.

The Process of Bibliotherapy With Children

Bibliotherapy can be an extremely useful tool when working with children.
A critical first step when using bibliotherapy in treatment is to match the appropriate book with the child experiencing problems. The child must be
able to see similarities between the self and the character in the book. An
important function of the clinician or helping person is to assist the child in
seeing similarities between the child's problem and the problem presented in
the book (Cianciolo, 1965). This initial stage of the bibliotherapy process is
identification and projection.
    When using bibliotherapy with older children or adults, the clinician can
further move the client to *abreaction and catharsis.* This stage is reached
when a client has an emotional release expressed verbally or nonverbally.
Once *abreaction and catharsis* have occurred, the clinician guides the client
into *insight and resolution* of the problem. As noted earlier, the bibliotherapeutic process is heavily grounded in Freudian theory—obviously, young
children are not capable of experiencing abreaction and catharsis leading to
insight into a problem in the traditional therapeutic sense.
    However, bibliotherapy does allow children to see solutions to problems
without the burden of in-depth verbalization, confrontation, and interpretation, all strategies often critical to successful therapy. With the guidance of
the therapist, the child is helped to identify with a character in a book having
a problem similar to his or her own. Through this process, the child begins
to see how the character in the book resolves a confronting problem, thus
recognizing possible solutions to his or her own problem with the help of
the therapist.
    Bibliotherapy with young children is necessarily a different process than
that used with older children and adults. The small vocabulary, problems

with verbalization, more limited range of experiences, and short attention span of children all impact the bibliotherapeutic process. The literature selected and the procedures used in treatment must be adapted to younger children, who cannot be confronted as directly as the adolescent or adult.

When conducting bibliotherapy with young children, the therapist must realize that reading an assigned piece of literature is out of the question for many of them. The alternative to assigned reading is for the therapist to read aloud to the child. One must keep in mind that the young child often cannot read, or if he or she is a troubled child, the child's reading skills may be poor.

Arbuthnot and Sutherland (1972) in their classic work *Children and Books* note the value of reading aloud to children from an educational point of view. The following quote would appear to be equally relevant to therapeutic intervention with children:

> As a teacher reveals her understanding and sympathy with the plights of fictional characters, she also reveals her potential of understanding and sympathy for the plights of the children in her class. As she reveals her delights in a vivid phrase or a fresh bit of imagery, she is also revealing something very personal about herself. It is an act of trust to which children are very responsive. Once that mutual trust is established, the child finds it easier to cope with threatening moments of tension. (p. 10)

A trusting bond between child and therapist is critical for therapy to be effective. Reading aloud provides an opportunity for a trusting relationship to develop between child and practitioner.

Whipple (1969) also notes that illustrations can facilitate the bibliotherapeutic process with young children:

> Illustrations may exert a negative as well as a positive appeal. The larger the total number of illustrations in the book, the higher the interest level. This point holds true up to an undefined point of saturation . . . The larger the average size of the illustrations, the higher the interest level, other things being equal. An illustration in several colors has greater merit than one that is black and white . . . An illustration with a center of interest that draws the eye to a particular point offers greater appeal to children than a picture with no recognizable center of interest or one subordinated by too many details. The more action and the more interesting the action, the more appealing is the illustration. The subject matter of the illustration has marked effect upon its interest to children. Eventful topics depicted in the illustration have greater merit than still life topics. (p. 195)

Cianciolo (1972) suggests that illustrations extend the child's world and help the child see that his or her wishes, feelings, and actions are often part of the normal growth process. Cianciolo concludes:

A picture is a window and it is through this window that the reader may
learn about individuals who live in an environment which differs from
his own. Illustrations constitute a powerful and pervasive means of
communicating a respect for the concept that minorities should not be
permitted to lose their identities in anonymity. One should appreciate the
challenge of being different . . . Each illustration should emphasize the
richness and diversity of the human experience, for it is especially in the
affective domain of the educative process that art leads the reader to a
better understanding of himself and others. (p. 56)

Peller (1962) reports that children are especially affected by illustrations
because such material nurtures daydreams. Peller concludes that animal
characters are especially useful because the factors of sex, age, and race are
not involved in the book; thus the child can concentrate on the content of the
story and on his or her daydreams.

Finally, when the helping person selects a book for treatment, a number
of critical guidelines should be followed. Young children obviously need a
much different book format from the older child. Six critical points identi-
fied by Gillespie and Connor (1975) are useful for selecting books for therapy with young children.

1. Appealing illustrations, whether pictures or photographs, that enhance
   the text and make good use of color.
2. Interesting story content, which presupposes a logical development of
   events and portrays believable characters.
3. Useful information, that is within the range of the child's understanding.
4. Broad humor, which needs to be fairly obvious for the young child.
5. Surprise elements, to create suspense and sustain interest.
6. Appealing, recurring refrains, which contribute familiarity and delight
   the child.

It must be noted that rarely will a book meet all of the above criteria.
However, the therapist should clearly keep each point in mind when selecting literature for children.

The Application of Bibliotherapy With Children

Once the practitioner has selected a book for treatment, decisions must be
made on how to best use the book in the therapeutic process. In order for
the child to identify with a story situation and with story characters, the
practitioner must encourage active participation in the literature on the part of
the child (Giblin, 1989). This participation may include activities making
use of motor skills, cognitive tasks, and verbal skills which follow the
reading of the book.

Reading Aloud

As pointed out earlier, bibliotherapy with young children is most successful when the book is read aloud. Even though a few precocious young children are good readers, the vast majority will better benefit if the book is read aloud. Consequently, the practitioner should select a book that will hold the child's interest and be relevant to the confronting problem.

It is critical that the practitioner read the book prior to its use in treatment. The helping person should give attention to the author's style, personality traits of book characters, unusual words or phrases in the book, and the illustrations used. The practitioner may wish to read the story aloud to him or herself before reading it to the child. This will help the practitioner emphasize important words and key punctuation marks. The practitioner should realize that level of pitch, tone of voice, and pace of reading are all critical to successful bibliotherapeutic intervention with children.

Observing Responses

When reading aloud, the practitioner must realize that many different kinds of responses will be observed in children. Children will respond in a spontaneous fashion to the story and are likely to become highly involved in the story emotionally. As they hear the story, children may criticize or applaud the story characters and even make value judgments about the characters. Anger, joy, envy, or relief may be expressed as the child hears the book read. These are all responses that the therapist should encourage and closely record because they are critical to the bibliotherapeutic process as well as successful treatment of the presenting problem.

Treatment Follow-up Activities

When using literature in treatment, often the practitioner only needs to read the book aloud and observe the child's responses. Many times the child will respond easily if the book selected interests the child; these responses will be shown in the child's comments or facial expressions. Some children, however, need more encouragement in responding to the literature presented. The practitioner may wish to use a number of follow-up activities to facilitate the bibliotherapy process. Follow-up activities encourage the child to make use of motor skills, cognitive abilities, and verbal skills. For example, the child over 4 years of age can draw representations of houses, people, animals, and other objects that are mentioned in the book. Likewise, role-playing is a useful activity that may help the child respond to problems that he or she cannot verbalize.

Often young children can construct collages and mobiles out of pictures or photographs which depict key events or activities in a story. Mood collages can also be effective in helping children better understand the emotions expressed by a story character.

The child can make puppets which help him or her express feelings about the story read. These can be constructed out of paper bags, socks, or small boxes. When children design the facial features of puppets, they should be encouraged to keep in mind the most important personality traits of the characters they wish to represent.

Written responses to the literature, although generally more effective with older children, can be adapted as a follow–up activity for young children. The young child can dictate to the therapist how he or she feels about a story character or situation. With younger children, dictation activities must be kept simple and involve a short time span. The child may wish to compose a letter to a book character, or create a different ending for a story; these activities place the child on a personal level with the story.

The practitioner must realize that various follow–up activities involving art, role–playing, and written responses can be effective as a means to identifying with a story character or situation. This participation of the child in the story can be a powerful factor in bringing about therapeutic change. Examples of follow–up activities and the application of bibliotherapy to problems are discussed in Chapter 2.

Limitations of Bibliotherapy

As with most therapeutic approaches, there are a number of limitations and precautions one should be aware of when using bibliotherapy. Probably the most important limitation to bibliotherapy is that it should never be used as a single approach to treatment; it is rather an adjunct to treatment (Pardeck & Pardeck, 1984, 1986).

As an art, bibliotherapy has a number of limitations. First, the empirical support for bibliotherapy conducted through fiction is mixed; however, the evidence suggests that nonfiction, in particular self–help books, does have sound scientific support in bibliotherapy. Secondly, many people are not inveterate readers; this means bibliotherapy has limited impact on this group. However, it has been pointed out that bibliotherapy can be conducted successfully with the nonreader through talking books as well as other innovative approaches. It must be noted that bibliotherapy appears to be most effective with children and adults who are in the habit of reading. It is also important that the helping person know the client well enough to judge the client's reading and interest levels. If the match between client and helper is incorrect, the reading material can frustrate the client (Pardeck & Pardeck, 1984).

Another limitation is that the client may intellectualize about a problem when reading about it. The client may fail to *identify* with a character in the story, resulting in a form of *projection* that only serves to relieve the client of any responsibility for resolution of a problem (Pardeck & Pardeck, 1984). Since younger children have limited cognitive development, this possibility is not as great.

Bernstein (1983) notes that there is a danger in relying on books too much. Bibliotherapy cannot solve all problems and may even reinforce fears, increase defenses, and promote rationalization in place of change. One must keep in mind that bibliotherapy is not a magical cure for all problems.

The possibility that the relationship with the helping person may be the cause of the resolution of a problem must also be considered (Zaccaria & Moses, 1968). As has been found for many therapeutic modalities, this can best be monitored by careful assessment of the effect of the therapeutic relationship versus the impact of bibliotherapy on the client's problem (Pardeck, 1990). If they keep the above limitations in mind, practitioners or other helping persons will find bibliotherapy to be a creative approach for dealing with problems confronting not only adults but also children.

References

Allen, R. D. (1978). An analysis of the impact of two forms of short-term assertive training on aggressive behavior. *Doctoral Dissertation: Southern Illinois University.*

Amato, A. (1957). Some effects of bibliotherapy on young adults. *Doctoral Dissertation: Pennsylvania State University.*

Appleberry, M. (1969). A study of the effect of bibliotherapy on third–grade children using a master list of titles from children's literature. *Doctoral Dissertation: University of Houston.*

Arbuthnot, M., & Sutherland, Z. (1972). *Children and books.* (4th ed.). Glenview, IL: Foresman.

Atwater, J. M., & Smith, D. (1987). Christian therapists' utilization of bibliotherapeutic resources. *Journal of Psychology and Theology,* **10,** 230–235.

Bailey, C. A. (1982). Effects of therapist contact and a self–help manual in the treatment of sleep–onset insomnia. *Dissertation Abstracts International* January through June 1983 (Vol. 43, Nos. 7-12).

Barker, R. L. (1987). *The social work dictionary.* Silver Springs, MD: NASW.

Barton, G. (1977). Treating marital conflict: The effects of bibliotherapy versus videotaped feedback and bibliotherapy on problem–solving behaviors in marital conflict. *Doctoral Dissertation: Brigham Young University.*

Baruth, L., & Burggraf, M. (1984). The counselor and single–parent families. *Elementary School Guidance and Counseling,* **19,** 30–37.

Baum, M. (1977). The short–term, long–term, and differential effects of groups versus bibliotherapy relationship enhancement programs for couples. *Doctoral Dissertation: University of Texas.*

Bernstein, J. (1983). *Books to help children cope with separation and loss.* (2nd ed.). New York: R. R. Bowker.

Berry, I. (1978). Contemporary bibliotherapy: Systematizing the field. In E. J. Rubin (Ed.), *Bibliotherapy Sourcebook* (pp. 185–190). Phoenix, AZ: Oryx Press.

Bigge, J., & Sandefur, J. T. (1960). An exploratory study of the effects of bibliotherapy on the behavioral pattern of adolescents. *Emporia, Kansas: Kansas State Teacher's College.*

Black, D. R., & Threlfall, W. E. (1986). A stepped approach to weight control: A minimal intervention and a bibliotherapy problem–solving program. *Behavior Therapy,* **17,** 144–157.

Black, M. J. (1981). The empirical evaluation of a self-administered conversational training Program. *Dissertation Abstracts International,* **42,** 1596B (University Microfilms No. 85-23, 265)

Bohlmann, N. R. (1986). Use of RET bibliotherapy to increase self–acceptance and self–actualization levels of runners. *Dissertation Abstracts International,* 46, 2191A. (University Microfilms No. 85–23, 265)

Caffee, C. L. (1975). Bibliotherapy: Its effects on self–concept and self–actualization. *Doctoral Dissertation: East Texas State University.*

Carr, R. (1975). The effects of bibliotherapy and modeling, videotaped feedback on problem–solving behaviors in marital conflicts. *Doctoral Dissertation: East Texas State University.*

Chambers, A. (1985). *Booktalk: Occasional writing on literature and children.* London: The Bodley Head.

Cianciolo, P. (1965). Children's literature can affect coping behavior. *Personnel and Guidance Journal,* **44,** 897–903.

Cianciolo, P. (1972). What can illustrations offer? In V. M. Read (Ed.), *Reading ladders for human relations.* (5th ed.). Washington, D C: American Council on Education.

Coleman, M., & Ganong, L. (1988). *Bibliotherapy with stepchildren.* Springfield, IL: Charles C. Thomas.

Coleman, M., & Ganong, L. (1987). The cultural stereotyping of stepfamilies. In K. Pasley & M. Ihinger–Tallman (Eds.), *Remarriage and stepparenting: Current research and theory* (pp. 19–41). New York: Guilford.

Conner, C. N. (1981). The effectiveness of bibliotherapy on teaching initiator dating skills to females. *Dissertation Abstracts International*, **42**, 3818B. (University Microfilms No. 82–03, 109)

Craighead, L., McNamara, K., & Horan, J. (1984). Perspectives on self–help and bibliotherapy: You are what you read. In S. Brown & R. Lent (Eds.), *Handbook of Counseling Psychology* (p. 918). New York: John Wiley and Sons.

Cuevas, J. L. (1984). Cognitive treatment of chronic tension headache. *Dissertation Abstracts International*, **46**, 955B. (University Microfilms No. 85–10, 012)

DeFrances, J., Dexter, K., Leary, T. J., & MacMullen, J. R. (1982). The effect of bibliotherapy and videotaping techniques on collective and self–concept formation in behaviorally disordered youth. *Proceedings of the 60th Annual International Convention of the Council for Exceptional Children*. Houston, TX. (ERIC Document Reproduction Service No. ED 218 885)

Dixon, A. (1988). Storyboxes: Supporting the case narrative in the primary school. *Cambridge Journal of Education*, 17, 151-156.

Dixon, J. (1974). The effects of four methods of group reading therapy on the level of reading, manifest anxiety, self–concept, and personal–social adjustment among fifth-and sixth–grade children in a central city school setting. *Doctoral Dissertation: State University of New York, Buffalo.*

Dodge, L. T., Glasgow, R. E., & O'Neill, H. K. (1982). Bibliotherapy in the treatment of female orgasmic dysfunction. *Journal of Consulting & Clinical Psychology*, **50**, 442–443.

Ford, J. D., Bashford, M. B., & DeWitt, K. N. (1984). Three approaches to marital enrichment: Toward optimal matching of participants and interventions. *Journal of Sex & Marital Therapy*, **10**, 41--48.

Frankel, M. J., & Merbaum, M. (1982). Effects of therapist contact and a self–control manual on nailbiting reduction. *Behavior Therapy*, **13**, 125–129.

Galliford, J. E. (1982). Eliminating self–defeating behavior: The effects of ESDB bibliotherapy compared to ESDB group therapy on weight control in women. *Dissertation Abstracts International*, **43**, 1978B. (University Microfilms No. 82–24, 784)

Giblin, P. (1989). Use of reading assignments in clinical practice. *The American Journal of Family Therapy*, **17**, 219–228.

Giles, L. P. (1986). Effects of reading–mediated vicarious reinforcement on the behavior of disturbed children. *Dissertation Abstracts International*, **47**, 4299B. (University Microfilms No. 87–02, 267)

Gillespie, M., & Connor, J. (1975). *Creative growth through literature for children and adolescents*. Columbus, OH: Merrill.

Glasgow, R. E., & Rosen, G. M. (1978). Behavioral bibliotherapy: A review of self–help behavior therapy manuals. *Psychological Bulletin*, **85**, 1–23.

Glasgow, R. E., & Rosen, G. M. (1979). Self–help behavior therapy manuals: Recent developments and clinical usage. *Clinical Behavior Therapy Review*, **1**, 1–20.

Griffin, B. (1984). *Special needs bibliography: Current books for/about children and young adults*. DeWitt, NY: Griffin.

Hannigan, M., & Henderson, W. (1963). Narcotics addicts take up reading. *The Bookmark*, **22**, 281–284.

Harbaugh, J. K., (1984). The effectiveness of bibliotherapy in teaching problem-solving skills to female juvenile delinquents. *Dissertation Abstracts International*, **45**, 3072A. (University Microfilms No. 84–29, 693)

Herminghaus, E. (1954). The effect of bibliotherapy on attitudes and personal and social adjustment of a group of elementary school children. *Doctoral Dissertation: Washington University*.

Jackson, E. (1944). Effects of reading upon attitudes toward the negro race. *Library Quarterly*, **14**, 47–54.

Kanaan, J. (1975). The application of adjuvant bibliotherapeutic techniques in resolving peer acceptance problems. *Doctoral Dissertation: University of Pittsburgh*.

King, N. (1972). The effects of group bibliocounseling on selected fourth –grade students who are underachieving in reading. *Doctoral Dissertation: University of the Pacific*.

Klingman, A. (1985). Responding to a bereaved classmate: Comparison of two strategies for death education in the classroom. *Death Studies*, **9**, 449–454.

Lewis, I. (1967). Some effects of the reading and discussion of stories on certain values of sixth–grade pupils. *Doctoral Dissertation: University of

California–Berkeley.

Libman, E., Fichten, C. S., Brender, W., Burstein, R., Cohen, J., & Binik, Y. M. (1984). A comparison of three therapeutic formats in the treatment of secondary orgasmic dysfunction. *Journal of Sex & Marital Therapy*, **10**, 147–159.

Link, M. (1977). The effect of bibliotherapy in reducing the fear of kindergarten children. *Doctoral Dissertation: Ball State University.*

Litcher, J., & Johnson, D. (1969). Changes in attitudes toward negroes of white elementary school students after use of multiethnic readers. *Journal of Educational Psychology*, **60**, 148–152.

Livengood, D. K. (1961). The effect of bibliotherapy upon peer relations and democratic practices in a sixth-grade classroom. *Doctoral Dissertation: University of Florida.*

Lundstein, S. W. (1972). A thinking improvement program through literature. *Elementary English*, **49**, 505–512.

Mackenzie, P. (1989). The contribution of "story" to children's development. *Early Child Development and Care*, **46**, 63-75.

Mattera, A. (1961). Bibliotherapy in a sixth grade. *Doctoral Dissertation: Pennsylvania State University.*

McClasky, H. (1970). Bibliotherapy with emotionally disturbed patients: An experimental study. *Doctoral Dissertation: University of Washington.*

McGovern, C. (1976). The relative efficacy of bibliotherapy and assertion training on the assertiveness levels of a general population and a library personnel population. *Doctoral Dissertation: Northwestern University.*

McKinney, F. (1977). Exploration in bibliotherapy. *Personnel and Guidance Journal*, **56**, 550–552.

Miller, D. L. (1982). Effect of a program of therapeutic discipline on the attitude, attendance, and insight of truant adolescents. *Dissertation Abstracts International*, 43, 1048A. (University Microfilms No. 82–20, 323)

Morris–Vann, A. M. (1983). The efficacy of bibliotherapy on the mental health of elementary students who have experienced a loss precipitated by parental unemployment, divorce, marital separation or death. *Dissertation Abstracts International*, **44**, 676A. (University Microfilms No. 83–15, 616)

Muehleisen, R. (1976). Reducing the risks of health change associated with critical life stress. *Doctoral Dissertation: Ohio University.*

Nesbitt, E. B. (1977). Comparison of two measures of assertiveness and the modification on nonassertive behaviors. *Doctoral Dissertation: University of Tennessee.*

Pardeck, J. A., & Pardeck, J. T. (1986). *Books for early childhood: A developmental perspective.* Westport, CT: Greenwood Press.

Pardeck, J. A., and Pardeck, J. T. (1984). *Young people with problems: A guide to bibliotherapy.* Westport, CT: Greenwood Press.

Pardeck, J. T. (1990). Children's literature and foster care. *Family Therapy,* **17,** 61–65.

Pardeck, J. T., & Pardeck, J. A. (1989). Bibliotherapy: A tool for helping preschool children deal with developmental change related to family relationships. *Early Child Development and Care,* **47,** 107–129.

Pardeck, J. T., & Pardeck, J. A. (1983). Using bibliotherapy in clinical practice with children of separation and divorce. *Arete,* **8,** 10–17.

Pardeck, J. T., & Pardeck, J. A. (1987). Using bibliotherapy to help children cope with the changing family. *Social Work in Education,* **9,** 107–116.

Peller, L. (1962). Daydreams and children's favorite books. In J. Rosenblith & W. Allensmith (Eds.), *The causes of behavior.* Boston, MA: Allyn and Bacon.

Penna, R. (1975). The relative effectiveness of the classroom discussion approach and the tutorial approach to literature for the development of adolescent ego–identity. *Doctoral Dissertation: Fordham University.*

Pezzot–Pearce, T. D., LeBow, M. D., & Pearce, J. W. (1982). Increasing cost–effectiveness in obesity treatment through use of self–help behavioral manuals and decreased therapist contact. *Journal of Consulting & Clinical Psychology,* **50,** 448–449.

Ponder, V. (1968). An investigation of the effects of bibliotherapy and teacher's self–others acceptance on pupils' self–acceptance and reading achievement scores. *Doctoral Dissertation: University of Southern Mississippi.*

Ray, R. D. (1983). The relationship of bibliotherapy, self–concept and reading readiness among kindergarten children. *Dissertation Abstracts*

International, **45**, 140A. (University Microfilms No. 84–02, 425)

Roach, L. E. (1975). The effects of realistic fiction literature upon the self–concept of elementary school students exposed to a bibliotherapeutic situation. *Doctoral Dissertation: University of Akron.*

Rosen, G. M. (1981). Guidelines for the review of do–it–yourself books. *Contemporary Psychology*, **26**, 189–91.

Rosen, G. M. (1987). Self–help treatment books and the commercialization of psychotherapy. *American Psychologist*, **42**, 46–51.

Rubin, R. (1978). *Using bibliotherapy: A guide to theory and practice.* Phoenix, AR: Oryx Press.

Rucker, J. P. (1983). An outcome study of two short–term weight loss methods: Bibliotherapy and interpersonal growth group therapy. *Dissertation Abstracts International*, **44**, 2421A.

Sadler, M. S. (1982). The effects of bibliotherapy on anomie and life satisfaction of the elderly: Literature, literary response, and the teaching of literature. Abstracts of doctoral dissertations published in *Dissertation Abstracts International*, January through June, 1983 (Vol. 43, Nos. 7–12). (ERIC Document Reproduction Service No. ED 230 983)

Saper, M. (1967). Bibliotherapy as an adjunct to group psychotherapy. *Doctoral Dissertation: University of Missouri.*

Schrank, F., & Engels, D. (1981). Bibliotherapy as a counseling adjunct: Research findings. *The Personnel and Guidance Journal*, **60**, 143–147.

Schultheis, M. (1972). *A guide for bibliotherapy.* Glenview, Il: Psychotechnics.

Schultheis, M. (1969). A study of the effects of selected readings upon children's academic performance and social adjustment. *Doctoral Dissertation: Ball State University.*

Shafron, P. W. (1983). Relationship between bibliotherapy and the self–esteem of junior high school students enrolled in remedial reading classes. *Dissertation Abstracts International*, **44**, 1037A (University Microfilms No. 83–18, 314)

Shearon, E. (1975). The effects of psychodrama treatment on professed and inferred self–concepts of selected fourth grades in one elementary school. *Doctoral Dissertation: University of Florida.*

Shirley, F. (1966). The influence of reading on the concepts, attitudes, and behavior of tenth–, eleventh–, and twelfth–grade students. *Doctoral Dissertation: University of Arizona.*

Shrodes, C. (1949). Bibliotherapy: A theoretical and clinical study. *Doctoral Dissertation: University of California.*

Smith, D., & Burkhalter, J. K. (1987). The use of bibliotherapy in clinical practice. *Journal of Mental Health Counseling,* **9**, 184–190.

Smith, N. B. (1948). Some effects of reading on children. *Elementary English,* **25**, 271-278.

Spache, G. (1974). *Good Reading for Poor Readers.* (9th revised ed.). Champaign, IL: Garrard Publishing.

Standley, F., & Standley, N. (1970). An experimental use of black literature at a predominantly white university. *Research in Teaching English,* **4**, 139–148.

Starker, S. (1986). Promises and prescriptions: Self–help books in mental health and medicine. *American Journal of Health Promotion,* **1**, 19–24, and 68.

Starker, S. (1988). Psychologists and self–help books: Attitudes and prescriptive practices of clinicians. *American Journal of Psychotherapy,* **42**, 448–455.

Stephens, J. (1974). An investigation into the effectiveness of bibliotherapy on the reader's self–reliance. *Doctoral Dissertation: University of Oklahoma.*

Swantic, F. M. (1986). An investigation of the effectiveness of bibliotherapy on middle grade students who repeatedly display inappropriate behavior in the school setting. *Dissertation Abstracts International,* **47**, 843A.

Tatara, W. (1964). Effects of novels on ideas about scientists. *Journal of Educational Research,* **58**, 3–9.

Taylor, V. W. (1982). An investigation of the effect of bibliotherapy on the self–concepts of kindergarten children from one–parent families. *Dissertation Abstracts International,* **43**, 3505A. (University Microfilms No. 83 –06, 465)

Tindall, W. (1986). Children's literature: A perspective. *Early Child Development and Care,* **26**, 229-251.

Tremewan, T., & Strongman, K. (1991). Coping with fear in early childhood: Comparing fiction with reality, *Early Child Development and Care*, **71**, 13-34.

Tucker, N. (1981). *The child and the book: A psychological and literary exploration.* Cambridge: Cambridge University Press.

Webster, J. (1961). Using books to reduce the fears of first–grade children. *Reading Teacher*, **14**, 159–162.

Webster's New Collegiate Dictionary. (1981). Springfield, MA: Merriam–Webster.

Whipple, C. (1978). The effect of short-term classroom bibliotherapy on the personality and academic achievement of reformatory inmate students. *Doctoral Dissertation: University of Oklahoma.*

Whipple, C. (1969). Practical problems of school selection for disadvantaged pupils. In J. Figurel (Ed.), *Reading and realism. Proceedings of the 13th Annual Convention of the International Reading Association.* Newark, DE., pp. 195–196.

Wilson, J. (1951). The treatment of attitudinal pathosis by bibliotherapy: A case study. *Journal of Clinical Psychology*, **7**, 345–351.

Zaccaria, J., & Moses, H. (1968). *Facilitating human development through reading: The use of bibliotherapy in teaching and counseling.* Champaign, IL: Stipes.

Chapter 2

Clinical Applications Of Bibliotherapy

Therapists who wish to use bibliotherapy to help children deal with problems must consider several factors when selecting books. The specific problem the child is facing is the most important factor in book selection. The child's interest and reading levels and alternate forms of book publication must also be considered.

As the earlier definition by Barker (1987) suggests, bibliotherapy can be useful for helping children deal with emotional problems, minor adjustment problems, or developmental needs. As this text will illustrate later, the helping person can locate books on many different problem areas facing children, including emotional and developmental needs.

The therapist must consider the child's interest and reading levels as well as the problem being faced by the child when selecting books for treatment. Chronological age and the level of maturity of the child largely determine the child's interest level. As to the child's reading level, a too-difficult book can greatly hamper the bibliotherapeutic process; likewise, a book with a reading level much lower than the child's may prove insulting.

Another consideration of book selection is the form of publication. Numerous books are available in paperback form, which is often more appealing to young children. Certain books have been developed in the forms of braille, large print, and talking books.

The last consideration in book selection is the decision of whether to use fiction or nonfiction in treatment. Some helping persons use informative nonfiction books for bibliotherapy purposes. For any of the stages of the bibliotherapeutic process to occur, however, the child reading the book must identify with a book character. Therefore, fiction books or nonfiction books with a biographical character seem to lend themselves most readily to the stages of the bibliotherapeutic process.

Principles of Bibliotherapy

Pardeck and Pardeck (1984, 1986) and Rubin (1978) outline the major principles of bibliotherapy as follows:

1. The helping person should use reading material which he or she is familiar with.
2. The helping person should be conscious of the length of the reading material. Complex materials with extraneous details and situations should be avoided.
3. The client's problem must be considered; the reading materials should be applicable to the problem but not necessarily identical to it.

27

4. The client's reading ability must be known and should guide the choice of reading materials used. If the client cannot read or has reading deficiencies, reading aloud or using audiovisual materials may be necessary.
5. The client's emotional and chronological age must be considered and reflected in the level of sophistication of the reading materials selected.
6. As Zaccaria and Moses (1968) note, reading preferences, both individual and general, are a guideline for selection:

> Reading preferences of children and adolescents go through a series of predictable stages. From the ages of 2 or 3 to about 6 or 7, children like to have stories read to them concerning familiar events. Then up to the age of 10 or 11 years, there is an increasing interest in fantasy stories. Adolescents, too, go through several reading stages. The early adolescent (12–15 years) tends to be interested in....animal stories, adventure stories, mystery stories, tales of the supernatural, sports stories....Later on (15–18 years), reading preferences change to such topics as war stories, romance, and stories of adolescent life. Perhaps sparked by the realization that maturity is fast approaching, the reading interests in late adolescence (18–21) tend to focus on such types of stories as those that deal with personal values, social significance, strange and unusual human experiences, and the transition to adult life.

7. Reading materials expressing the same feeling or mood as the client's are often good choices. This principle is called the "isoprinciple," which stems from the technique of music therapy and is commonly used in poetry therapy a well.
8. Audiovisual materials should be considered in treatment if reading materials are not available.

Treatment Approach to Bibliotherapy

The bibliotherapeutic process includes a series of distinct activities critical to using books in treatment. These include client readiness and book selection, as well as the client reading the book. Part of the therapeutic process is also to use follow–up activities. These activities are all aimed at moving the client through the stages of the bibliotherapeutic process: *identification and projection, catharsis and abreaction*, and *insight and integration.*

Readiness

Before proceeding with bibliotherapeutic treatment, the therapist or helping person must consider an important factor—the child's readiness. Inappropriate timing may impede the process. Normally, the child is most ready for the initiation of bibliotherapy when the following conditions have been met: (a) adequate rapport, trust, and confidence have been established by the therapist with the child; (b) if the client is an older child, the child and therapist have agreed upon the presenting problem(s); and (c) some preliminary exploration of the problem has occurred (Zaccaria & Moses, 1968).

Selection of Books

The therapist must consider several factors when selecting books for treatment. The most important factor is the presenting problem(s) of the child. The child may have a minor or major adjustment or developmental problem. Although books are available on virtually any problem, it is essential when using fiction that the book contain believable characters and situations offering realistic hope for the child. The therapist must also know the child's interest and reading levels.

One final element in book selection is the form of publication. Alternative forms such as braille, talking books (cassettes), and large type are available for special needs children. The therapist may wish to use a paperback edition because it may be more appealing to certain children (Fader & McNeil, 1968).

Introducing the Book

Once the child is ready for the bibliotherapeutic process and book selection has been completed, the therapist's next concern is how to introduce the book into treatment. Most helping persons feel it best to suggest books rather than to prescribe them if working with an older child; however, one may have to prescribe for the younger child. Regardless of what strategy the therapist uses for introducing the books into treatment, he or she must be familiar with the contents of the books selected.

Follow-up Strategies

Zaccaria & Moses (1968) conclude that there is virtual agreement among studies conducted on bibliotherapy: the reading of a book must be accompanied by discussion and/or counseling. During and after reading the book, the child may experience the three stages of the bibliotherapeutic process. Obviously younger children are not capable of experiencing abreaction and catharsis leading to insight into a problem in the traditional therapeutic sense. However, bibliotherapy does allow younger children to see solutions to problems without the in-depth verbalization, confrontation, and interpretation—strategies which are often critical to successful treatment. Instead, with the guidance of the therapist, the child is helped to identify with a book character having problems similar to his or her own. Through this process, the child begins to see how the character in the book resolves problems, and thus recognizes solutions (Pardeck, 1990). For older children, the advanced stages of the bibliotherapeutic process are possible with the help of the therapist (Pardeck & Pardeck, 1984).

The following activities can be utilized by a therapist or helping person after the book(s) have been read. These follow–up strategies are appropriate for most children. Certain follow–up activities require a small-group setting. The therapist can make use of one activity or several. The strategies include creative writing, art activities, discussion, and role-playing (Pardeck & Pardeck, 1984).

Creative Writing. After reading the book, the child might do the following:

1. Develop a synopsis of the book, using the point of view of a character other than the one who told the story.
2. Make a daily schedule or develop a time–line for the character in the story that the child identifies with, then compare to the child's own schedule or time–line.
3. Compose a diary for a character in the story.
4. Write a letter or a telegram from one character in the book to another, or from the child to one of the characters.
5. Create a different ending or stop reading before the last chapter and come up with an original ending.
6. Compose a "Dear Abby" letter that a character in the story could have written about a problem situation.
7. Write a news release concerning an incident in the book.

Art Activities. Art strategies are better suited to the child who enjoys artistic activities. The therapist may wish to follow up the reading of a book by having the child:

1. Make a map illustrating story events, with the child using his or her imagination to come up with details not given in the book.
2. Construct puppets or make soap or clay models of story characters and reenact a scene from the book.
3. Glue pictures and/or words cut from a magazine on a piece of cardboard to create a collage illustrating the events in the story.
4. Draw pictures in sequence or create a TV scroll of important incidents in the book.
5. Make a mobile that represents key events or characters in the book, using the child's own drawings or pictures cut from a magazine.

Discussion and Role-playing. The therapist may have the child:

1. Participate in a roundtable discussion concerning a decision one of the book characters is faced with.
2. Role-play an incident in the story, with the client taking the part of a key character.
3. Hold a mock trial concerning an incident in the story, with the clients playing the parts of defendant, lawyers, judge, jury, and witnesses.
4. Discuss the strong and weak points of a character the child identifies

with.

The helping person should, of course, keep in mind the child's maturity level and preferences when selecting follow-up activities. The therapist can adapt the activities to fit each child; for example, a child who dislikes writing can use a tape recorder for the creative writing activities. Depending on the child's problem and the type of book used, the therapist may wish to suggest several follow–up activities from which the child can select one or more.

Clinical Applications

The following two examples provide the reader with strategies to implement the bibliotherapeutic process with children confronted with divorce and child abuse. Please note that a number of books are recommended that the helping person might use in treatment. In the chapters which follow, detailed information is given on each of the books recommended.

Treating Children of Divorce

Many children are faced with the breakdown of their families due to divorce. Therapists who use bibliotherapy in treating children of divorce must be sure that the books used are realistic. For example, a book with a happy ending in which the parents reunite should be avoided (Rudman, 1976). It is also best to select books that do not blame a particular character in the story for family breakdown.

Helpful books on divorce must explore feelings and emotions, both positive and negative, that characters experience when their parents divorce. These emotions are typically bewilderment, unhappiness, and perhaps a sense of relief which is brought about when parents finally do break up. Books dealing with divorce should focus on coping with everyday problems of life after the divorce. Some of the major changes may be the financial situation of the family, a possible move, and added household responsibilities (Pardeck & Pardeck, 1984). It is helpful if books on divorce mention ways in which characters cope with the divorce; for example, a character might share problems with a friend who has also experienced divorce or might turn to a teacher or counselor for help (Pardeck & Pardeck, 1985).

The following books focus on children and divorce. They are used as illustrations for implementing the stages of the bibliotherapeutic process. It should be noted that these examples illustrate the initial stages of bibliotherapy; however, depending on the child's emotional and social development, skilled therapists can engage children in the advanced stages of the treatment process.

Zaccaria & Moses (1968) suggest that the mere reading of a book does not constitute bibliotherapy. Consequently, follow–up strategies to the reading are presented. The use of these and other creative approaches can aid in the older child's experiencing all of the stages of the bibliotherapeutic process.

In the following examples, the use of bibliotherapy is presented in both individual and group settings.

A therapist will find *Hey, That's My Soul You're Stomping on* (Corcoran,
1978) a helpful book for working with older children. Older children can
easily identify with 16–year–old Rachel, who spends the summer with her
grandparent awaiting the decision whether her parents will divorce or not.
When her parents do decide to divorce, Rachel is angry and wants to continue living with her grandparent, where she feels secure. Rachel eventually
reconsiders her decision, however, and returns to live with her mother. This
is an excellent book to use in a group setting. The therapist may ask a group
of older children who have experienced divorce to read the book and discuss it in a roundtable format. The discussion may deal with Rachel's decision to live with her mother. Some group members may wish to support the
decision; others may wish to support another possible living arrangement.

The helping person may wish to use the book *Don't Make Me Smile*
(Park, 1981) with younger children who have behavioral problems. A child
confronted with behavioral problems can easily identify with 10–year–old
Charles, the main character of the book. Charles refuses to attend school
and eventually runs away from home after his parents divorce. Charles finally returns home to live with his mother but resents her for telling him to
always cheer up. Charles also dislikes his father for divorcing his mother. A
child with behavioral problems might react very strongly to Charles's turmoil; this reaction can be used to help the child discuss his problems openly
with the helping person. The therapist may also have a troubled child write a
letter to Charles's mother and father. This will help the child express anger
at their lack of sensitivity toward Charles.

Children of divorce can be helped through the realistic book entitled *How
Does It Feel When Your Parents Get Divorced?* (Berger, 1977). Children of
divorce can easily identify with the young girl in this book as she describes
her life since her parent's divorce 2 years ago. A child with divorced parents
may experience projection after reading about how the girl in the book initially pretended that her parents would reunite, how she found herself
avoiding her friends, and how she resented her mother's dating.

The helping person might move the older child to abreaction and catharsis
by having the child compose a "Dear Abby" letter expressing the girl's
dilemma right after her parent's divorce. The child in the book finds that after 2 years have gone by, she thinks less about her parent's divorce and
more about other things she is interested in, such as friends and school. A
therapist might guide a child of divorce into insight and integration by having the child use pictures and words cut from a magazine to develop a collage illustrating his or her own outside interests.

These are but a few books available for helping children deal with divorce. By selecting books such as these for a young person confronted with
divorce and by using various follow–up activities, the therapist can help the
child deal with the many emotional issues associated with divorce. Finally,
the following case study provides in-depth detail of how the helping person
can support a child experiencing divorce.

A Case Example. The following case example illustrates the bibliotherapeutic process. The client, 8–year–old John, began having problems with schoolwork. The child appeared to be distraught and had problems interacting with other children. John's teacher referred him to the school social worker, who determined that John could benefit from counseling. The social worker decided to use bibliotherapy as a part of the therapeutic process. The first interview revealed that John lacked confidence in himself. The social worker noted the following comments John made during the interview: "I just can't do my school work" and "I am not smart enough." It was discovered that John's parents had divorced when he was 6. John's mother had recently remarried; consequently, John was having problems adjusting to his new family situation.

The social worker decided that the most pressing issue was to help John deal with the divorce of his parents. It was assumed that if he came to terms with the divorce, his problems related to schoolwork and interaction with other children would improve.

During a counseling session, the social worker introduced John to the book *What Kind of Family is This?* by Barbara Seuling (1985). This was accomplished by reading the book aloud to the child. The story is about a character named Jeff whose mother recently remarried. Jeff finds himself moving to a new house. Jeff still loves his biological father deeply and doesn't want another dad. He also hates sharing with his new stepsiblings. Jeff and his stepbrother even divide their bedroom in half, but later decide to fix up the room together. Jeff finds it just takes time to get used to his new family situation.

Even though 2 years had passed since John's parents had divorced, John was able to identify with the story character Jeff. The social worker had John dictate a letter about how the story character felt about moving to a new house and adjusting to a new family. This process gave insight into John's own feelings about his parents' divorce and his new blended family. After a number of treatment sessions, John gradually began to accept his parents' divorce and his new family situation. He also began to gain confidence in himself, and his schoolwork improved as well as his interaction with others.

Treating Child Abuse

Therapists who wish to use bibliotherapy with abused children must carefully select appropriate books. Child abuse is a extremely serious problem and must be treated with great caution when using bibliotherapy. Selected books should reflect as nearly as possible the abused child's familial situation and other critical circumstances related to the abuse. Matching story characters with the child's own experiences will help the child experience identification and projection.

Numerous children's books accurately depict problems found in the abusive family system. Generally, in these books only one child in the family is singled out for the abuse, and the nonabusive parent is often aware of the situation but does not interfere; this is a quite common situation in abusive families. Some of the books portray the abusive parent as chemically dependent or unemployed. The children in these books often feel ashamed and distrustful of adults and are afraid of telling anyone about the abuse. Reading about and reacting to any of these very realistic situations should lead the child to experience an emotional release with the help of the therapist.

Often the books on child abuse conclude with either the abused child or the abusive parent getting help, offering solutions that an abused child may be able to apply directly to his or her own situation. Other books have vague endings, not always pleasant, that can lead to important open–ended discussion between the child and helping person concerning alternative strategies for solutions to the problem. With the guidance of the therapist, books can thus assist the maltreated child in experiencing insight and integration by developing new ways of dealing with the problems associated with abuse.

The following section overviews several excellent books that deal with the problem of child abuse. They appeal to various age groups and family situations. Most of these books are available in school or public libraries.

The problem of sexual abuse is realistically portrayed in *Fair Game* (O'Hanlon, 1977). This book is about a 14–year–old girl named Denise who dislikes her alcoholic stepfather; he spies on her when she is in the shower and begs her not to tell anyone. She suffers from nausea whenever she thinks about her stepfather, and her grades and schoolwork begin to suffer. Denise's mother is oblivious to the stepfather's frequent drunkenness, and she cannot understand why Denise is having problems in school. After she gets her mother to recognize her stepfather's alcoholism, Denise is able to concentrate on her schoolwork. Denise discovers, however, that her stepfather has made sexual advances toward one of her friends and even her younger sister. Denise's mother forces her husband to leave and feels guilty about what has happened to her daughters.

The book *Margaret's Story* (Anderson & Fine, 1986a) is an excellent portrayal of sexual abuse. Margaret must go to court because she has been victimized. Initially she is afraid to inform her parents about the sexual abuse, because the perpetrator told her to remain silent about it. Margaret finds out that what was done to her is against the law.

The War of Villa Street (Mazer, 1978) focuses on child abuse and alcoholism. Willis, an eighth-grader, has always been an outsider. His family has moved frequently, and he has always been teased by his friends about his alcoholic father. Willis's only outlet is running just for the fun of it. After beating Willis practically unconscious one evening, Willis's father is horrified at the bruises he sees on Willis the next day and vows to stop drinking. Over the next few weeks things seem to be looking up; however, a gang Willis refuses to join beats him up. Willis tries not to let the gang bother him; he even enters a running event. When Willis's drunken father comes to the event, Willis is embarrassed by his presence and is unable to win. At home afterward, Willis's father begins to beat him, and Willis strikes back. Willis runs away from home but soon returns, determined to be recognized for his accomplishments and not his father's behavior.

The book *Gunner's Run* (Orr, 1980) focuses on the problem of a child being cared for by an alcoholic father. Gunner is frequently beaten by his father, sometimes to the point of unconsciousness. When Gunner's older sister runs away to California, Gunner decides he must escape his father as well. An old man takes Gunner in, and the two become good friends. When Gunner contacts his father, he is beaten again by him. The older man with whom Gunner stays becomes ill, and Gunner feels a great sadness when the man dies. Gunner, who has developed a better self–concept through his friendship with the old man, doesn't know what he will do but hopes his older sister will return.

Break in the Sun (Ashley, 1980) presents a simple story about Patsy, a 12–year–old girl who is both physically and emotionally abused by her stepfather. Patsy's mother, busy with a new baby, doesn't stand up for Patsy. Patsy starts to wet the bed at night, which greatly embarrasses her. After Patsy meets an older girl involved with a touring summer theater company, she decides to run away from them. Distraught over Patsy's disappearance, Patsy's mother informs the police, but they are unable to help. Patsy's stepfather and her only friend take a train in search of Patsy. When they find Patsy, her attitude toward her stepfather begins to change.

There are many excellent books on child abuse; the above examples are only a few. The following case example illustrates how the therapist can use bibliotherapy with the abused child (Pardeck, 1990).

Case Example. For bibliotherapy to be effective, the therapist must explore the child's reaction to the book. Young children may naturally comment on book illustrations while being read to. Older children may mention main characters of a book. The therapist can use discussion to guide the child toward identification with certain aspects of a book character's situation or with feelings the book characters are expressing. However, the therapist can use numerous other activities to further involve the child in the story. These activities include art, written responses, and dramatization.

In the following case example, bibliotherapy is implemented through a group approach. Such a strategy can serve as an effective adjunct to other supportive therapies, including individual and family.

The case example (Pardeck, 1990) describes a group of children who were abused. The group met on a weekly basis for 6 weeks and was conducted by a therapist who had extensive knowledge of bibliotherapy and children's literature. The purpose of the group was to provide support, improve socialization skills, and raise the self–esteem levels of the children.

Because the children were all 6 and 7 years old, they had limited reading skills. Thus the practitioner read the books out loud to the group. The books used during the group sessions were *Fly Free* (Adler, 1984) and *Michael's Story* (Anderson & Finne, 1986b). These two books are ideal for young children; they accurately portray the problem of abuse as seen through the eyes of a child.

During the first and second sessions of treatment, *Fly Free* was read aloud to the children by the therapist. The children simply listened; they did not respond to the book. This kind of response was expected, because abused children often show caution toward adults; also, young children have limited verbalization skills.

During the third session, the children began to respond to the book. During this session, the practitioner asked the group to write a letter to the child in *Fly Free*. This was accomplished by having the children verbalize all the things they would like to tell the story character who had been abused. The therapist wrote all of their ideas down on paper and created the letter. Through this process, the children were able to begin identifying with the story.

In the fourth session, the practitioner read *Michael's Story*. After hearing the story, the children created three simple masks to represent feelings of happiness, sadness, and anger. Then portions of the story were reread aloud by the practitioner, with each child holding up the appropriate mask for the feeling displayed by the story character. This activity enabled the children to experience feelings about having been a victim of abuse.

In the final two group sessions, each child was asked to create a story about the characters in *Fly Free* and *Michael's Story*. The practitioner recorded their stories during the fifth group session and read each story out loud during the final group session. This process not only helped the children verbalize additional emotions about their victimization as they reacted to the stories, but also appeared to contribute to their socialization skills. All of the children benefited from the bibliotherapy experience. The benefits of bibliotherapy included improvement in the interaction skills of the children with their peers and adults. Children were also better able to verbalize feelings about their victimization. Clearly, verbalization enhanced the well–being of the children.

Conclusion

Practitioners must realize that bibliotherapy cannot be used with all children, in all settings, or for all purposes. Therefore, the practitioner needs to use good judgment in the application of bibliotherapy. This chapter offers ways in which bibliotherapy can be applied to practice. It has been suggested that books are useful not only for helping children to identify emotions which may be troubling but also to help practitioners establish trust with children they are working with. As suggested, positive therapeutic reaction to the story includes identification with a character, followed by a cathartic discussion of story events. Through this process, the practitioner can help the child develop insight into a problem, which hopefully leads to resolution of the problem.

Helpful points to consider when choosing books for bibliotherapy include colorful illustrations that nurture daydreams, and animal characters that do not involve issues of gender, age, ethnicity, and social class. As suggested in this chapter, younger children after reading the book do best when asked to draw pictures of places and characters, role-play situations, make collages, and construct puppets. Older children prefer to use writing projects to assimilate feelings, such as composing letters or writing different endings to books. Finally, it should again be emphasized that bibliotherapy is an adjunct to other therapies and should be viewed as providing creative alternatives within the therapeutic relationship.

References

Adler, C. S. (1984). *Fly Free*. Esst Rutherford, NJ: Coward–McCann.

Anderson, D., & Finne, M. (1986a). *Margaret's story*. Minneapolis: Dillion Press.

Anderson, D., & Finne, M. (1986b). *Michael's story*. Minneapolis: Dillion Press.

Ashley, B. (1980). *Break in the sun*. New York: S. G. Phillips.

Barker, R. L. (1987). *The social work dictionary*. Silver Springs, MD: NASW.

Berger, T. (1977). *How does it feel when your parents get divorced?* New York: Julian.

Corcoran, B. (1978). *Hey, that's my soul you're stomping on*. New York: Atheneum.

Fader, D. N., & McNeil, E. B. (1968). *Hooked on books*. New York: Berkeley.

Mazer, H. (1978). *The war on villa street*. New York: Delacorte Press.

O'Hanlon, J. (1977). *Fair game*. New York: Dial Press.

Orr, R. (1980). *Gunner's run*. New York: Harper and Row.

Pardeck, J. A., & Pardeck, J. T. (1986). *Books for early childhood: A developmental perspective*. Westport, CT: Greenwood Press.

Pardeck, J. A., & Pardeck, J. T. (1984). *Young people with problems: A guide to bibliotherapy*. Westport, CT: Greenwood Press.

Pardeck, J. T. (1990). Bibliotherapy with abused children. *Families in Society*, **70**, 229-235.

Pardeck, J. T., & Pardeck, J. A. (1985). Bibliotherapy using a neo–Freudian approach for children of divorced parents. *School Counselor*,

32, 313–318.

Park, B. (1981). *Don't make me smile*. New York: Knopf.

Rubin, R. (1978). *Using bibliotherapy: A guide to theory and practice.* Phoenix, AR: Oryx Press.

Rudman, M. (1976). *Children's literature: An issues approach.* Lexington, MA: Health.

Seuling, B. (1985). *What kind of family is this?* Racine, WI: Western Publishing.

Zaccaria, J., & Moses, H. (1968). *Facilitating human development through reading: The use of bibliotherapy in teaching and counseling.* Champaign, IL: Stipes.

Chapter 3

Changing Role Models

Children through the socialization process acquire their individual and sexual identity. While the family has the greatest influence on the development of children's identity, the school, neighborhood, and community also play an important role in this developmental process. Presently, all of these systems are experiencing social change; children thus may have problems related to identity development (Collins, Ingoldsby, & Dellman, 1984).

The process through which children acquire their individual and sexual identities has been explained by three major theories--learning, psychoanalytic, and cognitive-developmental theories. In all of these, parents play a critical role; however, each has a different interpretation of the role of parents (Samuels, 1977).

Bandura (1969) is one of the leaders in the area of learning theory. He argues that children acquire their individual and sexual identities through the learning process. Bandura concludes that sex-role is established early through the following process: a) immediately after birth, a name indicative of the child's sex is given; b) the child is often encouraged to dress in sex-typed clothing and is given sex-typed toys to play with; and c) role appropriate behaviors from the child are usually reinforced by the parents. In other words, sex-role training starts at birth, when appropriate sexual responses are rewarded and sex-inappropriate behaviors are punished (Mussen, 1969). Through this process, the child gradually begins to identify with the appropriate gender role and also develop his or her individual identity.

Psychoanalytic theory offers a much different view. Even though parents are seen as central figures to the child's developing his or her identity, the process through which this happens is much different than what learning theorists believe. Psychoanalytic theory presents a complex intrapsychic process that links sexual identity to the resolution of the Oedipus Complex for boys and the Electra Complex for girls. According to the Oedipus Complex, the boy fears that his father will castrate the child in retaliation for the child's loving feelings for his mother. Since the child realizes he cannot win the struggle for his mother, he resolves the Oedipus Complex by identifying with his father. The Electra Complex is similar to the Oedipus Complex in that the female child feels a strong sexual attraction to her father (Santrock, 1983). Because these desires are inappropriate and would result in punishment, they create anxiety in the child. The child is able to suppress these inappropriate feelings and reduce anxiety through identification with her mother. It should be stressed that the above offers a greatly condensed presentation of the sexual identification process as understood through psychoanalytic theory.

The cognitive-developmental theory concludes that love and affection for the parents by the child bring about the child's individual and sexual identity. It is the child's conception of his or her body and how it differs from

others that greatly determines the child's identification with the male or female sex-role. This process begins when the child is initially labeled "boy"
or "girl." The label becomes the central organizer for the child's life and determines many of the child's activities, values, and attitudes. Once the child
has stabilized gender identity, the child positively values those objects consistent with this identity and acts in accordance. This process provides the
child with cognitive consistency.

According to cognitive-developmental theory, a child's stereotypes of
masculine and feminine behavior are not derived from reinforcement or
identification but from universal, perceived sex differences in bodily structure and capacities between males and females (Mussen, 1969). The child's
developing understanding of cultural sex-roles and cognitive development
are major factors in the creation of the child's sexual behavior. This behavior helps to determine how the child perceives the self.

It must be clearly noted that none of the above theories provides a defini-
tive answer to why and how children develop their individual and sexual
identities. Learning, identification, and cognitive development all probably
contribute to the overall socialization process impacting the child's development of self. One might be safe in concluding that the first components of
one's identity are learned through reinforcement and imitation and that identification and cognitive growth become more important as the child grows.
Even though the process is far from clear, all three theories do suggest that
parents and the family system are critical to this developmental process.
Since there has been a major change in parenting roles and the family system over the last 2 decades, children may have problems related to the identification process. Specifically, within families the division of labor between
parents is not always clear and indeed, in many families, the female or male
role may not even be present due to family breakdown. One must note that
all major theories of sex-role development suggest that both males and females play a role in children's developing identity. If one parent is absent
from the family, it is far from clear how the process plays out.

Gilligan (1982) argues that all of the major theories explaining child development are problematic because they are created from a male perspective.
For example, it has been argued that the Freudian theory of human development has a tendency to be damaging to women. Furthermore, Erickson
(1968), a neo-Freudian, focuses mainly on masculine development and
dedicates limited discussion to feminine development. Chodorow (1978)
concludes that the masculine bias of psychoanalytic theory suggests that
women have weaker ego boundaries and that they are more prone to mental
illness. Instead, Chodorow (1978) replaces Freud's negative and derivative
view of female psychology with a positive view of her own:

Girls emerge with a stronger basis for experiencing another's needs or
feelings as one's own (or of thinking that one is so experiencing another's needs and feelings). Furthermore, girls do not define themselves in
terms of the denial of preoedipal relational modes to the same extent as
do boys. Therefore, regression to these modes tends not to feel as much

a basic threat to their ego. From very early, then, because they are parented by a person of the same gender . . . girls come to experience themselves as less differentiated than boys, as more continuous with and related to the external object world, and as differently oriented to their inner object-world as well. (p. 167)

Thus, Chodorow concludes that relationships, and particularly issues of dependency, are experienced differently for males and females. For females, issues of femininity do not depend on the achievement of separation from the mother or on the process of individuation. For males, separation and individuation are aspects of identity, since separation from the mother is essential for the development of masculinity. Finally, Chodorow (1978) concludes that in all societies, women define the self in terms of relationships and connectedness to other people; males do not.

The work of Chodorow (1978) and Gilligan (1982) must be considered carefully when one attempts to understand gender development. They suggest that masculine psychology has persistently and systematically misunderstood women and their motives, including their psychological growth and development. Obviously, the theories of Chodorow and Gilligan have important implications for parents and others who work with children.

The changing occupational structure of industrial society plus the evolving roles of females and males have led to consideration of a new developmental concept called "androgyny." This word comes from two Greek words, andros (male) and gyne (female), and is often defined as "being sex-role flexible" (Santrock, 1983). The concept of androgyny has emerged as an alternative to traditional sex roles, because the belief that masculinity and femininity are opposites is being refuted by many social scientists. A number of studies generally conclude that sex-roles should not be viewed as bipolar sexual extremes, but rather as dualistic dimensions within each other (Santrock, 1983). The implications of an androgynous sex-role orientation for understanding child development is significant. Research suggests that children with androgynous characteristics are highly valued by society (Santrock, 1983), appear to have increased levels of achievement and high self-esteem, and are found to be caring and warm individuals (Pardeck & Pardeck, 1987). Given the positive view of society toward androgynous child development and the research findings concerning this concept, therapists may wish to take this information into account when working with children experiencing problems related to identification. In terms of the field of bibliotherapy, numerous books are now available that deal with problems related to individual and sexual identification, family change, and androgyny.

References

Bandura, A. (1969). Social learning theory of identification process. In D. A. Goslin, (Ed.), *Handbook of socialization theory and research.* Chicago: Rand McNally.

Chodorow, N. (1978). *The reproduction of mothering*. Berkeley: University of California Press.

Collins, L. J., Ingoldsby, B. B., & Dellman, M. M. (1984). Sex-role stereotyping in children's literature: A change from the past. *Childhood Education*, **60**, 278-285.

Erikson, E. (1968). *Identity: Youth and Crisis*. New York: W. W. Norton.

Gilligan, C. (1982). *In a different voice*. Cambridge, MASS: Harvard University Press.

Mussen, P. H. (1969). Early sex role development. In D. A. Goslin, (Ed.), *Handbook of socialization theory and research*. Chicago: Rand McNally.

Pardeck, J. T., & Pardeck, J. A. (1987). Using bibliotherapy to help children cope with the changing family. *Social Work in Education*, **14**, 107-116.

Samuels, S. C. (1977). *Enhancing self-concept in early childhood: Therapy and practice*. New York: Human Sciences Press.

Santrock, J. W. (1983). *Life-span development*. Dubuque, IA: William C. Brown.

Books on Changing Role Models

Adler, Susan (Editor). *Mightier Than the Lipstick: Stories By Women*. London: Viking, 1990. IL: Ages 14-18.

A collection of feminist stories for teenagers, including a wide range of work from all over the world.

Ahlberg, Allan. *Miss Brick the Builder's Baby*. London: Puffin, 1981. IL: Ages 3-7.

A story about a woman who is a builder.

Ahlberg, Allan. *Miss Dose the Doctor's Daughter*. London: Puffin, 1987. IL: Ages 3-7.

A story about a woman who is a medical doctor.

Ahlberg, Allan. *Mrs. Plug the Plumber*. London: Puffin, 1980. IL: Ages 3-7.

A story about a woman who is a plumber.

Alda, Arlene. *Sonya's Mommy Works*. New York: Little Simon, 1982. IL: Ages 4-6.

Sonya loves weekends because she doesn't have school and can spend lots of time with her parents. Since her mother has gone back to work, Sonya has made several adjustments. She needs to be independent with dressing herself and preparing snacks. Sonya has a babysitter who cares for her after school; her father spends more time with her. When Sonya's mother leaves town for several days as part of her job, Sonya is very unhappy. She gets lots of attention from her grandmother and father; however, she is glad when her mother returns.

Anderson, Karen. *What's the Matter, Sylvie, Can't you Ride?* New York: Dial Press, 1981. IL: Ages 4-6.

Sylvie becomes frustrated and frightened when she tries to learn to ride her new birthday bike. When Sylvie's friends and her mother glide by on their bikes, she kicks her new bike and abandons it. After she goes back to get her bike the next day, she mistakenly starts down a hill and finds she has to pedal to stay on.

Asch, Frank. *Good Horsey*. Englewood Cliffs: Prentice-Hall, 1981. IL: Ages 2-4.

During her father's nightly ritual of preparing her for bed, a young girl imagines that he turns into a horse. After the girl takes an adventurous ride, the horse slowly turns back into her father, who resumes putting her bed.

Asch, Frank. *Just Like Daddy*. Englewood Cliffs: Prentice-Hall, 1981. IL: Ages 2-4.

A very young bear spends his day imitating all activities his father engages in. The mother joins them on a fishing trip. Father catches a small fish, but the little bear catches a big fish just like his mother's.

Bang, Molly. *Ten, Nine, Eight*. London: Puffin, 1983. IL: Ages 1-4.

A counting lesson and bedtime story shared by a young girl and her father, rich with tenderness.

Barbato, Juli. *From Bed to Bus*. New York: Macmillan, 1985. IL: Ages 4-6.

A girl has problems bathing, brushing her teeth and dressing each morning as she gets ready for school. With help from her parents and siblings, she is able to find a way to overcome each obstacle. Even though she can now get ready for school, she still has trouble getting to the bus on time.

Bauer, Caroline. *My Mom Travels a Lot*. New York: Frederick Warne, 1981. IL: Ages 4-6.

A small girl's mother must travel because of her job. The girl lists the good and bad points about the situation. Although she greatly misses her mother, the child and her father develop a close relationship and share the household responsibilities when the mother is gone on trips.

Berenstain, Stan and Berenstain, Jan. *The Berenstain Bears and Mama's New Job*. New York: Random House, 1984. IL: Ages 4-6.

When Mama Bear is urged to turn her quilt-making hobby into a business, she rents an empty store much to her family's surprise. Once Mama Bear begins spending time at work, Papa and the bear children find they must be more self-reliant and help Mama with the household chores. Although the whole family has some adjustments to make, it is worth it because Mama Bear is so happy.

Bradshaw, Jane. *Out To Lunch*. London: Puffin, 1992. IL: Ages 14-18.

This book shows different men and women sitting in a cafe. The role expectations of men and women are illustrated through their take, appearance, and behavior.

Brandenberg, Franz. *Otto Is Different*. New York: Greenwillow Books, 1985. IL: Ages 4-6.

Otto, who is an octopus, laments the fact that he is so different from his friends because of his many arms. His wise parents point out the advantages of having eight arms; he can get dressed and do his chores four times as fast. After a successful hockey game playing goalie, Otto is convinced that being different from others isn't so bad and may prove to be quite advantageous.

Buckley, Helen. *Someday With My Father*. New York: Harper and Row, 1985. IL: Ages 5-7.

Sitting in her nightgown and looking out the window, a small girl dreams of someday being with her father.

Caple, Kathy. *The Biggest Nose*. Boston: Houghton Mifflin, 1985. IL: Ages 4-6.

Eleanor, who is an elephant, becomes quite self-conscious about her large nose when her classmates tease her about it and try to measure it. At home Eleanor twists her nose into a knot in an effort to shorten it. Although her parents and older sister try pulling and oiling her nose in attempts to loosen the knot, only Eleanor's sneeze releases the knot. Thankful to have her nose back to normal, Eleanor points out to her classmates the next day that each has different characteristics—biggest mouth, longest tail, and other features.

Cartwright, Ann, and Cartwright, Reg. *Norah's Ark*. London: Puffin, 1983. IL: Ages 3-8.

Life at Puddle Farm was blissful except for the pond which was much too small. But the rain soon changed all that. This story portrays a female farmer.

Chevalier, Christa. *Spence Isn't Spence Anymore*. Chicago: Albert Whitman and Company, 1985. IL: Ages 4-6.

When Spence declares that he is tired of being Spence, his mother gives him fuzzy ears and a tail so that he can be Somebody Else. Somebody Else spends the day doing all the things Spence usually did, but the next day Somebody Else is surprised to discover that mother is wearing a disguise and is now Big Somebody Else. Spence does not like the stranger and Big Somebody Else wishes Spence would return, so they both remove their disguises and become son and mother again.

Cohen, Miriam. *No Good in Art*. New York: Greenwillow Books, 1980. IL: Ages 4-6.

Jim is convinced that he cannot draw or paint well. A teacher encourages everyone to be creative and is able to say something positive about each child's drawing. Jim finds out that he can do art and that others are interested in his work.

Cohen, Miriam. *So What?* New York: Greenwillow Books, 1982. IL: Ages 4-6.

A boy worries that he cannot perform well on the jungle gym. He also cannot dance well. A friend advises him that everyone is different, with certain tasks being easier for some children than for others. He is finally able to perform well on the jungle gym and his dance improves, thus helping the boy to accept himself.

Cole, Babette. *Princess Smartypants*. London: Hamish Hamilton, 1986. IL: Ages 4-7.

This princess enjoys being a Ms. who successfully frightens off all potential husbands.

Cooney, Nancy. *The Blanket That Had to Go*. New York: Putman's Sons, 1981. IL: Ages 4-6.

A girl is very attached to an old blanket which is her constant companion. When her mother announces that she cannot take her blanket to kindergarten, the girl is in despair until she comes up with a plan. A week before kindergarten begins, her brother cuts the blanket in half for her; by the first day of school, it has unraveled until it is pocket size.

Davis, Gibbs. *Katy's First Haircut*. Boston: Houghton Mifflin, 1985. IL: Ages 4-6.

Katy's long hair is always in the way, so she gets a haircut. Once her hair is cut, however, she wants it back. She eventually finds that there are real advantages to having short hair, and she reassures a friend about to get a haircut.

Davis, Gibbs. *The Other Emily*. Boston: Houghton Mifflin, 1984. IL: Ages 4-6.

A girl named Emily writes her name everywhere and possesses a nightlight and T-shirt bearing her name. She is surprised and outraged on her first day of school when she discovers that there is another Emily in her class. Her parents are sympathetic when she claims she is no longer special. She finally becomes friends with the other Emily. The girl realizes she is still unique even though she has the same name as her friend.

De Jong, Meindart. *Isn't She Clever?* London: Puffin, 1991. IL: Ages 7-10.

This book makes an anti-sexist point. The mother's unwaged activity is paralleled with a paid job.

Delton, Judy. *I Never Win!* Minneapolis: Carolrhoda Books, 1981. IL: Ages 4-6.

Charles repeatedly loses races and games to his peers. He becomes very discouraged. To ease his anger, he practices the piano for hours at a time. When his piano teacher requests that he play for her guests and he is applauded loudly, Charles feels he has finally won at something important.

Duffy, Carol Ann (Editor). *I Wouldn't Thank You For a Valentine*. London: Viking, 1992. IL: Ages 14-18.

An international collection of contemporary poetry by women aimed at teenagers.

Frankel, Alona. *Once Upon a Potty*. Woodbury, NY: Barron's Educational Service, 1980. IL: Ages 2-4

A boy named Joshua and his mother are introduced in this book. The mother describes the functions of various parts of the body. Expressing her weariness at diaper changing, she is pleased when Joshua receives a potty. Joshua explores various uses for the potty, but discovers its main purpose is for elimination. It is stressed that potty training is a slow process and even though children continue to have accidents, they will finally succeed.

Galloway, Priscilla. *When You Were Little and I Was Big*. Toronto: Annick Press, 1984. IL: Ages 2-6.

A little girl imagines that she is the adult and her mother, a child. The girl describes what she would do as an adult: never get mad when awakened early, take the child to work, play pretend with the child and always read extra stories each night. The girl describes herself as a good parent, just like her mother.

Greenberg, Polly. *I Know I'm Myself Because. . .* New York: Human Sciences Press, 1981. IL: Ages 4-6.

A young girl discusses her identity. She is aware of her growing body, the range of emotions she feels, and of her physical abilities. By exploring how she is like other children and how she is different, the child realizes her uniqueness within her family and in school.

Greene, Bette. *Get On Out of Here, Philip Hall*. London: Puffin, 1981. IL: Ages 8-12.

Beth's competitive streak sometimes gets the better of her, but her spirit and energy and her organizational ability is never questioned. Beth wants to be a veterinarian when she grows up.

Greene, Bette. *Philip Hall Likes Me, I Reckon Maybe*. London: Puffin, 1979. IL: Ages 8-12.

A story about a bright, black school girl, growing up in the mid-southern United States. Beth, the main character, wants to be a veterinarian.

Gregory, Philippa. *Princess Florizella*. London: Viking, 1988. IL: Ages 5-8.

This book is about a princess who is not pretty and has strong feminist ideals. She does not marry and is able to remain happy.

Haddon, Mark. *A Narrow Escape for Princess Sharon*. London: Hamish Hamilton, 1989. IL: Ages 5-8.

Sharon is a princess who enjoys playing football and listening to music but doesn't want to get married to creepy Count Colin.

Hardcastle, David. *Joanna's Goal*. London: Blackie, 1992. IL: Ages 6-9.

Joanna is as good or better than most boys at football. She must persuade Craig, the captain of the Colts team, that she can play well.

Hemmings, Susan (Editor). *Girls Are Powerful*. London: Plus, 1982. IL: Ages 14-18.

A collection of pieces written by young women from seven to twenty-two about issues affecting girls and young women.

Henkes, Kevin. *Clean Enough*. New York: Greenwillow Books, 1982. IL: Ages 4-6.

As a boy soaks in a bathtub, he remembers when his father used to bathe him and he decides he must be growing bigger because the tub seems smaller. Now he's too busy playing and pretending to take time to wash himself. He assumes he is clean enough when his mother calls for him to get out of the bathtub.

Hines, Anna. *All By Myself*. Boston: Houghton Mifflin, 1985. IL: Ages 2-4.

A small girl convinces her mother that she no longer needs to wear a diaper at bedtime. The girl wakes up in the night, and her mother helps her go to the restroom. She has an accident one night, followed by nights where she wakes her mother up time and again to go to the restroom. One night she is not able to wake her mother, and the girl is able to use the restroom on her own.

Hines, Anna. *Daddy Makes The Best Spaghetti*. New York: Ticknor and Fields, 1986. IL: Ages 3-5.

A boy and his father enjoy a close relationship that is aptly demonstrated in picture and story. The story uses humor to illustrate the relationship.

Ives, Penny. *Mrs. Christmas*. London: Hamish Hamilton, 1992. IL: Ages 3-7.

It is time for Christmas presents to be delivered, but Father Christmas and his reindeer are ill. Mrs. Christmas is both willing and able to take over.

Jones, Charlotte Folz. *Only Child—Clues For Coping*. Philadelphia: Westminister, 1984. IL: Ages 10-13.

This story accentuates the positive aspects in an effort to air the pluses and minuses of being an only child.

Keller, Holly. *Geraldine's Blanket*. New York: Greenwillow Books, 1984. IL: Ages 2-6.

Very attached to her baby blanket, Geraldine the pig takes it everywhere and helps wash and mend it. When her parents decide she is too old to carry around a blanket, they successfully try to hide it and then try to replace the blanket with a new doll. Still adamant about wanting her blanket near her, Geraldine solves the problem by making clothes for her new doll out of the blanket.

Kemp, Gene. *The Turbulent Term of Tyke Tiler*. London: Puffin, 1979. IL: Ages 8-12.

An anti-sexist book that helps children explore gender expectations and assumptions.

Kempler, Susan, Rappaport, Doreen, and Spirn, Michele. *A Man Can Be . . .* New York: Human Science Press, 1981. IL: Ages 4-6.

A father and his young son spend the day together with such activities as preparing a meal, visiting a playground, and getting ready for bed. A man's ability to express many emotions ranging from anger to nurturing is stressed. The boy's father is seen as a friend as well as a caring adult and role model for the child.

Leaf, Munro. *The Story of Ferdinand*. London: Puffin, 1987. IL: Ages 5-8.

The story of the bull who does not like to fight, but instead likes flowers.

Leiner, Katherine. *Both My Parents Work*. New York: Watts, 1986. IL: Ages 7-10.

Nine children who have families in which both parents work talk about what their parents do and, as a result, how their own days are structured.

Levenson, Kath. *When I Grow Up and You Grow Down*. New York: Lothroop, Lee, and Shepard, 1983. IL: Ages 4-6.

A girl imagines all of the benefits she would have if she switches roles with her mother. She could go out for the evening, she could order her mother to clean her bedroom, she could eat sweets and snacks while her mother ate nutritious food. When the girl considers having no one tuck her into bed, brush her hair, or comfort her when she's hurt, she decides that perhaps it's best to remain a child for a while.

Long, Earlene. *Gone Fishing*. Boston: Houghton Mifflin, 1984. IL: Ages 2-4.

In preparing for a fishing trip, a father eats a big breakfast and gets his big fishing rod while his young son eats a small breakfast and finds his little fishing rod. The two spend the day together fishing and eat lunch. They are surprised when the little boy catches a big fish as well as a small one and the father catches a big and small fish, too.

Magorian, Michelle. *Back Home*. London: Viking, 1985. IL: Ages 8-12.

Twelve year-old Rusty, who had been evacuated to the United States when she was seven, returns to the grey austerity of post-war Britain. Rusty's mother is a mechanic.

Mahy, Margaret. *Keeping House*. London: Hamish Hamilton, 1991. IL: Ages 3-8.

Lizzie is far too busy at her job to keep her house tidy. She seeks the services of Robin Puckertucker the Wonder Housekeeper to clean her home.

Mahy, Margaret. *The Man Whose Mother Was a Pirate*. London: Puffin, 1972. IL: Ages 2-4.

A funny story about a quiet man and his outrageous pirate mother.

Mark, Jan. *Hairs on the Palm of My Hand*. London: Puffin, 1982. IL: Ages 8-12.

Two stories showing just what life in a modern school can be like. The main character, Eileen, challenges sexism in the school and gets a lot of people thinking.

McPhail, David. *Pig Pig Grows Up*. New York: E. P. Dutton, 1980. IL: Ages 2-6.

As the youngest in his family, Pig Pig refuses to grow up. He eats baby food, wears baby clothes, throw tantrums, and sleeps in a crib. Pig Pig's parents finally give up on encouraging him to grow up. When he is faced with an emergency, he decides to grow up very quickly and is a hero afterwards.

Mitchell, Joyce. *My Mommy Makes Money*. Boston: Little, Brown, and Company, 1984. IL: Ages 4-6.

Mothers are shown with various occupations, including jobs that are traditionally male-oriented such as carpenter, appliance repair person, surgeon, and minister. In the book children visit their mothers at work, while all show pride in their mother's accomplishments.

Moncure, Jane Belk. *Now I Am Two!* Chicago: Children's Press, 1984. IL: Ages 2-4.

A 2-year-old proudly describes physical skills as well as cognitive accomplishments.

Newman, Alyse. *It's Me, Claudia!* New York: Franklin Watts, 1981. IL: Ages 4-6.

Claudia is unhappy with the size of her ears and unsuccessfully tries to tape and paste them down. She is pleased when she discovers that her mother's hat will hide her ears; however, the hat covers most of her face as well, causing her to be accident prone. When friends don't recognize her with the hat on, Claudia decides to remove the hat and accept her appearance.

Ormerod, Jan. *Dad's Back*. New York: Lothrop, Lee, and Shepard, 1985. IL: Ages 2-4.

A baby delights in father's return and explores what dad has brought back from his trip. Then the two play and chase each other about.

Oxenbury, Helen. *Mother's Helper*. New York: Dial Press, 1982. IL: Ages 2-4.

A toddler is shown helping mother with household chores and learning to play independently.

Parish, Peggy. *I Can–Can You? (Levels 1, 2, 3, 4)* New York: Greenwillow Books, 1980. IL: Ages 2-6.

A series of progressively more difficult physical and social skills are presented. Toddlers are illustrated in Level 1 waving good-bye, playing peek-a-boo, as well as other activities. Level 2 focuses on such activities as block playing and mastering eating and drinking skills. In Level 3 bathroom skills, running, and jumping skills are presented. Sharing, saying please and thank-you, bathing, and dressing are all covered by preschoolers in Level 4.

Pearson, Susan. *Everybody Knows That!* New York: Dial Press, 1978. IL: Ages 4-6.

Although their peers try to convince them differently, best friends Herbie and Patty enjoy playing together with trains and trucks as well as with dolls.

Pomerantz, Charolette. *Posy*. New York: Greenwillow Books, 1983. IL: Ages 4-6.

A small girl and her father spend quality time together, with him telling her stories about when she was a toddler. The stories stress her parents' warmth and caring attitude, with respect shown for the girl's decisions as a child.

Provensen, Alice and Provensen, Martin. *A Peaceable Kingdom: A Shaker Abecedarius*. London: Puffin, 1978. IL: Ages 3-7.

This is an illustrated alphabet rhyme book that includes animals from alligator to zebra. The book shows educated women, making evident the Shaker belief in sexual equality.

Robinson, Deborah. *Bye-Bye, Old Buddy*. New York: Clarion Books, 1983. IL: Ages 4-6.

Jenny dearly loves her baby blanket but realizes she has outgrown it. Jenny considers burying the blanket, raffling it off, or attaching balloons to it and letting it float away. She finally mails the blanket to an address that she randomly selects from the phone book. The person who receives the blanket puts it to good use as a puppies' bed.

Rosen, Michael (Editor). *Culture Shock*. London: Plus, 1990. IL: Ages 14-18.

A collection of papers dealing with the issue of gender and equality for women.

Schwatz, Amy. *Bea and Mr. Jones*. Scarsdale, NY: Bradbury Press, 1982. IL: Ages 4-6.

Tired of kindergarten activities, a girl agrees to trade places with her executive father for one day. She loves the hectic pace of her father's advertising job, and her father excels in his kindergarten subjects. Both are so happy with their new roles, they decide to make the roles permanent.

Sebestyan, Ouida. *Words By Heart*. London: Hamish Hamilton, 1968. IL: Ages 14-18.

Lena is a young black girl growing up against a background of prejudice and threatened violence in the American South. The story presents the problems of racism and sexism.

Shyer, Marlene Fanta. *Here I Am, An Only Child*. New York: Scribner's 1985. IL: Ages 4-6.

A boy considers the pros and cons of being an only child.

Simon, Norma. *Nobody's Perfect, Not Even My Mother*. Chicago: Albert Whitman and Company, 1981. IL: Ages 4-6.

A group of children realize that no one is perfect--not even the adults in their lives, such as teachers, parents, and grandparents. However, just as each of the adults has an area he or she excels in, so do the children. Even though children make mistakes, all have a special achievement that should give him or her pride.

Sirof, Harriet. *The Real World*. New York: Watts, 1985. IL: Ages 11-14.

Cady Stanton's mother is a staunch feminist, and Cady subscribes to her views that marriage enslaves women, that people are more important than things, and that doing what's right is more important than getting ahead.

Spotts, Audra. *Standing Ovation*. New York: Berkley/Ace/Tempo, 1983. IL: Ages 11-15.

Fifteen-year-old Darlene is feeling lost as a middle child in a family of six, so she decides to get away from the pack by pursuing her interest in a musical instrument.

Stecher, Miriam, and Kandell, Alice. *Daddy and Ben Together*. New York: Lothrop, Lee, and Shepard, 1981. IL: Ages 4-6.

A boy and his father share many activities, yet they find it difficult to adjust when the child's mother is away from home with her new job. The child pouts because his father runs the household differently and always seems tired. When they go on a picnic and spend the day together, the child and his father realize that they can make it on their own when the mother is gone.

Stones, Rosemary and Mann, Andrew. *Mother Goose Comes to Cable Street*. London: Puffin, 1989. IL: Ages 3-7.

A collection of twenty rhymes with detailed illustrations showing multi-ethnic, multi-cultural working-class London, with women and men, girls and boys, in unstereotyped roles. Some rhymes are familiar; others are not.

Szekeres, Cyndy. *Thumpity Thump Gets Dressed*. Racince, WI: Western Publishing, 1984. IL: Ages 2-4.

A small rabbit exhibits his prowess at dressing when he dons a variety of clothing and outer garments during the course of a day. It seems that each time he dresses to go outside, the weather changes and he must switch clothing. As the rabbit prepares for bed, he assures his father that he can dress for any type of weather he wishes.

Tester, Sylvia Root. *Frustrated, Jealous, Sad*. Chicago: Albert Whitman and Company, 1980. IL: Ages 4-6.

A child explores feelings and shares problems with a caring adult.

Titherington, Jeanne. *Big World, Small World*. New York: Greenwillow Books, 1985. IL: Ages 4-6.

A girl and her mother spend Saturday together. Their experiences during the day are different because of their age differences. The mother looks at her face in the mirror, while the girl checks her toes. The girl drinks milk while the mother drinks coffee. However, at the end of the day they both come home and give the girl's father a kiss and a hug.

Tyler, Linda. *When Daddy Comes Home*. New York: Viking/Kestrel, 1986. IL: Ages 3-5.

A story for every child whose father does not work typical hours.

Ure, Jean. *A Proper Little Nooryeff*. London: Plus, 1983. IL: Ages 14-18.

Jamie thinks ballet is pretty wet, until he encounters Anita and discovers there is more to ballet than meets the eye.

Van Woerkom, Dorothy. *Something To Crow About*. Chicago: Albert Whitman and Company, 1982. IL: Ages 4-6.

Ralph the rooster embarks on single parenthood when he decides to hatch a basketful of orphaned eggs.

Vestly, Anne-Cath. *Hallo Aurora*. London: Puffin, 1966. IL: Ages 5-8.

A story about a Swedish family where the mother works and the father looks after the house.

Vigna, Judith. *Daddy's New Baby*. Chicago: Albert Whitman and Company, 1982. IL: Ages 4-6.

During a weekend spent with her father and stepmother, a young girl is initially jealous of their new baby but later helps her father care for the baby.

von Konigslow, Andrea. *Toilet Tales*. Toronto: Annick Press, 1985. IL: Ages 2-4.

The story gives explanations for why different kinds of animals could never use a toilet; for example, a giraffe couldn't fit through the door, an elephant would smash it, a seal would slip off. A toilet is described as appropriate only for big girls and boys.

Walsh, Ellen. *Theodore All Grown Up*. Garden City, NY: Doubleday and Company, 1981. IL: Ages 4-6.

A boy decides that he has become a grown-up overnight. He decides he has all of the privileges of an adult. His parents advise him to give away all of his toys, so he sorts through them and decides he does not want to give them up. He concludes that he is not a grown-up yet but has grown a little bit.

Walter, Mildred. *Justin And The Best Biscuits in The World*. New York: Lothrop, 1986. IL: Ages 6-8.

This story is a portrayal of African-American family life. A young boy learns that it doesn't matter who works, men or women, when it needs to be done.

Wandro, Mark, and Blank, Joani. *My Daddy Is A Nurse*. Reading, MA: Addison-Wesley, 1981. IL: Ages 4-6.

The focus of this book is on fathers who have occupations usually associated with women. Along with a description of their work, daddies are illustrated who are preschool teachers, librarians, ballet dancers, and flight attendants. The book concludes with a father who is a homemaker busy caring for children and house.

Watanabe, Shigeo. *Daddy, Play With Me!* New York: G. P. Putnam's Sons, 1984. IL: Ages 2-4.

A young bear and his father become involved in play. The boy and his father seem to equally enjoy dancing, sharing a piggyback ride, playing horse, and becoming a train and airplane together. The father and son grow tired and take a nap.

Watanabe, Shigeo. *How Do I Put It On?* New York: G. P. Putnam's Sons, 1980. IL: Ages 2-4.

A small bear demonstrates that he is able to dress himself with no help from his parents.

Watson, Wendy. *Jamie's Story*. New York: Philomel, 1981. IL: Ages 2-4.

Mother and father share the cooking and child care responsibilities, with their toddler gladly assisting.

Weiss, Nicki. *Hank and Oogie*. New York: Greenwillow Books, 1982. IL: Ages 4-6.

Hank as a baby receives a stuffed hippo, and the two become inseparable friends for the next few years. Hank is too embarrassed to take his stuffed hippo to kindergarten; however, he still eats with him at home and sleeps with him. The boy finally decides he can do his daily routines without the stuffed hippo and places the animal on a shelf with other toys he has outgrown.

Wells, Rosemary. *Benjamin and Tulip*. London: Viking, 1973. IL: Ages 6-9.

Whenever Benjamin passes Tulip's house she beats him up, until he finally takes the situation in hand.

Winthrop, Elizabeth. *Tough Eddie*. New York: E. P. Dutton, 1985. IL: Ages 4-6.

A small child likes to play cowboys because it makes him feel tough. He becomes embarrassed, however, when his older sister tells her friends that he has a dollhouse in his closet. When the boy stands still until a bee flies off him, everyone in his class at school admires his bravery. Feeling more secure, he even considers bringing his dollhouse to show at school the next day.

Ziefert, Harriet. *Zippety Zip!* New York: Viking Press, 1984. IL: Ages 2-4.

A boy takes pride in being able to dress himself, brush his teeth and wash his face.

Zolotow, Charlotte. *William's Doll*. New York: Harper and Row, 1972. IL: Ages 4-6.

Although his father insists on giving William masculine toys, a sensitive grandmother realizes the young boy's need for a doll and gives him one to care for.

Chapter 4

Blended Family

Most men and women who divorce eventually remarry. A large proportion of remarriages involve children. The transition into a blended family, a family system created from elements of other broken families, is not always a smooth one. Many children have considerable difficulty in adjusting to their new blended families and stepparents.

The research literature on blended families is limited. However, several studies have given insight into the special problems experienced by the children of blended families.

Age of children appears to be an important factor in determining their adjustment to the blended family. Younger children seem to adjust more readily to the blended family than older children, while the adolescent has the greatest problem in adjustment. Children from families broken by divorce versus the death of a parent have better adjustment in the blended family (Walter & Stinnett, 1971).

An obvious problem in the blended family is the complex role structure. The child in the blended family is likely to have stepsiblings, stepparents, stepuncles, and stepgrandparents. Some children have problems adjusting to these new immediate and extended family members. Role confusion is often a problem in the blended family (Duberman, 1975). For example, during holidays or birthdays, the complex role structure within the blended family can result in role confusion and anxiety for children. The children may have to celebrate special days at two or more different households, involving people they may see no more than once a year. A child's birthday may well turn into a complex and frustrating situation because of role confusion.

A major problem related to role confusion in the blended family is that stepparents may have difficulty in completely assuming the parenting role. One clinical study found that regardless of how hard the stepparent tries to be a parent for the stepchild, numerous problems always appear to be present (Fast & Cain, 1966). A child, for example, may say during an argument, "My real father would never get mad at me the way you always do." Even if the stepparent tries to be the ideal parent, the child will often continue to idolize the absent biological parent.

Another problem is that stepparents may share the parental role with a previous parent. The stepparent may feel he or she can completely replace the biological parent from whom the child has separated. The stepparent can easily become resentful when this expectation is not fully realized. This situation adds tension to the relationship with the stepchild. Bernard (1956) found considerable resentment of men and women in blended families toward their stepchildren: one third of divorced men and 44% of divorced women were found not to be affectionate toward stepchildren.

Other factors that create problems between children and stepparents are associated with family roles. One major issue is the expectation by stepparents that their stepchild should automatically love them because they are now a family. The stepchild is likely to resent the new parent and may feel he or she will never love the stepparent. Even if the child makes an effort to love the new parent, the stepparent may negatively misinterpret these loving emotions and consequent behavior.

Another problem of role functioning and confusion related to stepparenting is that the parent may have problems assuming the new parenting role. In particular, the stepparent may have a tendency to favor his or her biological children over his or her stepchildren. This will often result in familial conflict. In turn, the competition and rivalry between stepchildren is at times problematic within the blended family.

Fuller (1988) has summarized the research on blended families in a recent article. She reports general agreement in the research suggesting that younger children adjust more readily to the blended family than older children. Children adjust better to the blended family after the death of the biological parent versus divorce. Children deal more effectively with blended families if there is cooperation and support among spouses and former spouses. Fuller concludes that the strengths of blended families are often overlooked. She suggests that blended families can: a) provide additional siblings for learning and enjoyment, b) teach children conflict-resolution skills, c) increase children's happiness with parents, d) improve the standard of living for children, e) increase the number of people who care about the children, f) expose children to multiple role models, and g) promote flexibility in children because they must adjust to new situations.

Kupisch (1984) concludes that practitioners can improve the functioning of blended families by helping them to achieve the following six tasks:

1. *Finding realistic, appropriate roles models for stepparents.* The role of parent in the blended family is different from the role of parent in first marriages. The role of parent in the blended family is largely negotiated; both adults and children must learn to clarify and understand the role of stepparent.

2. *Redefining financial and social obligations.* Even though a marriage may end, the financial responsibility for children continues. Also, stepparents must realize that social relationships which existed prior to the blended family still remain.

3. *Arranging custody and visitation patterns.* Finding ways to allow children to maintain contact with both parents requires planning and flexibility. Arguments and custody battles over visitation rights are not uncommon in blended families, and children are often the pawns.

4. *Establishing consistent leadership and discipline.* Open communication is critical for maintaining consistency in discipline techniques due to the increased number of authority figures and two households. Controversy over discipline approaches and divided loyalties may well be one of the more stressful areas experienced by children in blended families.

5. *Dispelling myths and tempering idealism.* Practitioners can help

stepparents understand that love of stepchildren is not automatic and often requires patience and time.

6. *Forming emotional bonds within the blended family.* Time and work are needed to develop emotional bonds for all members of blended families. Parents must have a quality relationship, and children must feel a sense of security within the blended family.

Finally, it is critical for practitioners working with blended families to be sensitive to the attitudes and beliefs about these families. In particular they must realize that all families have strengths and weaknesses, and that the blended family is no exception to this rule. The following annotated books capture many of the problems associated with blended families. These include role conflict and confusion as well as unrealistic expectations stepparents and children often have of each other. Many of the strengths of blended families, however, are also emphasized. These include teaching children how to adjust to change and providing them with the opportunity to form new and loving relationships.

References

Bernard, J. (1956). *Remarriage: A study of marriage.* New York: Dryden Press.

Duberman, L. (1975). *The reconstituted family: A study of remarried couples and their children.* Chicago: Nelson-Hall Company.

Fast, I., & Cain, A. (1966). The stepparent role: Potential for disturbances in family functioning. *American Journal of Orthopsychiatry*, **36**, 485-490.

Fuller, M. (1988). Facts and fiction about stepfamilies. *Education Digest*, **54**, 52-54.

Kupisch, S.(1984). Stepping in--to counseling with stepfamilies. *The Virginia Counselors Journal*, **12**, 38-43.

Walter, J., & Stinnett, N. (1971). Parent-child relationships: A decade of research. *Journal of Marriage and the Family*, **33**, 70-116.

Books on The Blended Family

Adler, C. .S. *Footsteps on the Stairs*. New York: Delacorte, 1982. IL: Ages 10-14.

Thirteen–year old Dodie, whose mother seems to always be criticizing her, has become very fond of her new stepfather Larry. Therefore, she does not look forward to her stepfather's two children visiting them during the summer. Both girls are in competition for Larry's attention, with Anne's younger brother seeming to be the only one happy with the situation. In solving a mystery, the two stepsisters grow closer, and Dodie and her mother talk about how to improve their relationship. The summer ends with plans for Larry's children to spend more time with him, Dodie, and her mother.

Adler, C. S. *In Our House Scott Is My Brother*. New York: Macmillan, 1980. IL: Ages 11-14.

Jodi and her father have lived alone for 3 years since her mother's death. When her father suddenly remarries, Jodi finds herself with not only a new stepmother but also a 13–year-old stepbrother. Scott is an embarrassment to Jodi at school, where they totally avoid each other. They talk at home, however, and Scott confides that he's a shoplifter. Jodi also discovers that her stepmother has a drinking problem. Just when the new marriage starts to look shaky, Jodi and Scott realize they've become good friends.

Ashley, Bernard. *Break in the Sun*. New York: S. G. Phillips, 1980; London: Puffin, 1980. IL: Ages 11-14.

Patsy, a girl around 12 years old, has been desperately unhappy ever since her mother remarried. Patsy's stepfather verbally and physically abuses her, and Patsy's mother, busy with a new baby, doesn't stand up for her. Patsy has even started wetting the bed at night, which greatly embarrasses her. When Patsy meets an older girl in a touring summer theater group, Patsy decides to run away with them. Patsy's stepfather and Patsy's only friend, Kenny, take a train in search of Patsy. Kenny dislikes Patsy's stepfather, but after talking with the man, Kenny better understands him. Patsy's stepfather was beaten himself as a boy and frequently ran away from home. When her stepfather and Kenny find Patsy, she feels trapped and prepares to jump from a high structure. At the last minute, sensing a different attitude from her stepfather, Patsy descends to start over again with him.

Bates, Betty. *Bugs in Your Ears*. New York: Holiday House, 1977. IL: Ages 11-14.

Thirteen–year-old Carrie is disappointed when her mother gets remarried. Carrie's new stepfather has three children of his own, and it's crowded when they all move into a house together. Carrie has to attend a different school, where she's in the same class as one of her stepbrothers. Carrie's stepsiblings seem to dislike her and feel that Carrie's mother is trying to take over. When Carrie's new stepfather insists on adopting her, she grows even more resentful. Eventually, all the children realize what a strain their parents are under and save their money so the whole family can celebrate their parents' 1–month anniversary.

Bates, Betty. *Thatcher Payne-in-the-neck*. New York: Holiday House, 1985. IL: Ages 9-12.

Kib and Thatcher, longtime friends at their summer lake cottages, develop a plan to get their parents married to each other. Things go as planned; however, they have second thoughts after the marriage.

Berger, Terry. *Stepchild*. New York: Julian Messner, 1980. IL: Ages 8-11.

David, a young boy whose parents have been divorced for 2 years, is upset when his mother announces her plans to remarry. David still wishes his parents could get back together. At his mother's wedding, David meets his new stepbrother and stepsister and senses that they are unhappy as well. David resents the changes in his life after his mother remarries but eventually comes to the realization that it is possible to love his stepfather without taking away from the close relationship he maintains with his father.

Betancourt, Jeanne. *Puppy Love*. New York: Avon/Camelot, 1986. IL: Ages 1-13.

Aviva alternately spends 1 week with her mother and her new stepfather, and 1 week with her father. This movement back and forth between homes presents problems for her.

Boyd, Lizi. *The Not-So-Wicked Stepmother*. London: Puffin, 1989. IL: Ages 3-7.

Hessie discovers that her dad's new wife isn't as wicked, mean, and ugly as the stepmothers in her storybooks.

Bradley, Buff. *Where Do I Belong? A Kid's Guide to Stepfamilies*. Reading, MA: Addison-Wesley Publishing, 1982. IL: Ages 12-18.

According to this book, both parents and children have adjustments to make and fears to face when entering a stepfamily. Sharing holidays or special events and coexisting as a household with different standards are two of the many problems discussed, with suggestions for coping.

Breslin, Theresa. *Different Directions*. London: Puffin, 1989. IL: Ages 14-18.

A story about a girl who has enough problems without her mother joining her at school. The girl thinks her mother is having a romance with a teacher.

Burt, Mala Schuster, & Burt, Roger B. *What's Special About Our Stepfamily? A Participation Book For Children*. New York: Doubleday, 1983. IL: Ages 9-12.

This book is about a new stepfamily as told through the eyes of a 10-year-old child. The book includes fill-in-the-blank questions, illustrations that can be colored, and space for drawing or writing down thoughts.

Clifton, Lucille. *Everett Anderson's 1-2-3*. New York: Holt, Rinehart, and Winston, 1977. IL: Ages 5-8.

Everett, a young black child, thinks that one is a lonely number but two is just right, with he and his mother doing things together. He is a little worried about his mother starting to like Mr. Perry, because Everett thinks the apartment might get too crowded if Mr. Perry were always there. During a walk, Mr. Perry tells Everett that he doesn't expect to take his daddy's place but wants a chance to be himself. Everett decides that the number three may work out just fine.

Craven, Linda. *Stepfamilies: New Patterns in Harmony*. New York: Messner, 1982. IL: Ages 12-18.

Utilizing vignettes in introducing each chapter, the book discusses the many types of problems and conflicts that arise in Stepfamilies.

Drescher, Joan. *My Mother's Getting Married*. New York: Dial, 1986. IL: Ages 6-10.

In picture-book format, Drescher covers the problems in society when a child resents a parent's remarriage.

Duncan, Lois. *The Twisted Window*. London: Hamish Hamilton, 1987. IL: Ages 12-14.

Because of Brad's charm and good looks, Tracy agrees to help him kidnap his half-sister back from his stepfather.

Eyerly, Jeannette. *The Phaedra Complex*. New York: J. B. Lippincott, 1971. IL: Ages 14-18.

Laura, a high school junior, feels everything is changed when her mother gets remarried. She has difficulty attending her mother's wedding and is resentful that she will be left behind during the honeymoon. Once her mother and stepfather return, however, Laura's life falls into a pattern. She can't understand why her new stepfather appears so jealous of a boy she meets and is so upset when Laura comes in late from a date. Laura's mother and stepfather begin to argue frequently. After her mother takes an overdose of pills and refuses to let Laura visit her at the hospital, Laura realizes that the relationship between herself and her stepfather has visibly been getting out of bounds. It takes much time for the three of them to reestablish themselves as a family, and it is decided that Laura should go away to school.

Francis, Dorothy. *The Flint Hills Foal.* Nashville: Abingdon, 1976. IL: Ages 8-11.

Ten–year-old Kathy dislikes her new stepbrother Jay and feels as if her new stepmother is constantly scolding her. Feeling distanced from her father as well, Kathy begins spending time at a horse ranch helping the owner. When a foal runs away, Kathy rescues it and nurses it back to health. When Kathy discovers that Jay is afraid of horses, she better understand Jay's teasing and bragging. Kathy realizes she has also misinterpreted some of her stepmother's actions and that Jay and his mother want to include Kathy in their new family.

Getzoff, Ann, and McClenahan, Carolyn. *Stepkids: A Survival Guide for Teenagers in Stepfamilies.* New York: Walker, 1984. IL: Ages 12-18.

This book presents examples of problems in Stepfamilies from the viewpoint of the teenager. It is suggested that older children more so than younger children have the power to improve the functioning of the blended family. Practical suggestions are offered for dealing with the blended family.

Green, Phyllis. *Ice River*. Reading, MA: Addison–Wesley, 1975. IL: Ages 8-14.

Dell lives with his mother and stepfather. Dell's father often fails to show up for his promised Sunday visits, and when Dell discovers that his mother is pregnant, he feels all alone except for his pet dog. When Dell's dog jumps into the river and cannot be found, on the same day that his mother has a miscarriage, the double loss is too much. Dell cries in his stepfather's arms, sad about at the changes in his life and the realization that his father will probably never visit him again. Dell's stepfather seems to understand, and the two are happy when Dell's dog returns home that night.

Greene, Constance C. *Al (exandra) the Great*. New York: The Viking Press, 1982. IL: Ages 11-14.

Thirteen–year-old Alexandra and her friend pack in preparation for Al's trip to visit her father and stepmother. Al feels angry about her father's remarriage and she is reluctant to leave her divorced mother. She worries about her mother always being tired because of long hours at work. When Al's mother is put in the hospital with pneumonia, Al has to stay with her friend. The two girls argue and discover they envy each other—Al because her friend has a stable family life and her friend because Al gets to go on trips to visit her father. Al decides it's her responsibility to care for her mother after her hospital stay. She reluctantly calls her father to cancel her vacation plans and is pleased when he and her stepmother tell Al how proud they are of her.

Greene, Constance C. *Getting Nowhere*. New York: The Viking Press, 1977. IL: Ages 11-14.

Mark, 14, resents his father's remarriage, while his 12–year-old brother likes their new stepmother. Mark feels left out of his dad and stepmother's plans each weekend. Mark is especially jealous of the new car his dad buys for her and makes a long scratch mark on its side. He becomes more hostile when his father hits him during an argument. When Mark takes his younger brother and a friend for a joyride in his stepmother's car and has an accident injuring the two other boys, his dad and stepmother consider sending him to a psychiatrist.

Greene, Constance C. *I and Sproggy*. New York: The Viking Press, 1978. IL: Ages 8-11.

Ten–year-old Adam, who lives with his divorced mother, is glad when his father and new stepmother move into his neighborhood. However, Adam hates the idea of sharing his father with his stepsister Sproggy, also 10. Adam is rude to Sproggy and is furious when his friends ask her to join their club. Adam's mother is supportive about his problem but leaves the solution up to him. When some neighborhood girls tease Sproggy, he comes to her rescue. Sproggy is grateful and does a favor for Adam as well, making him realize that having a stepsister isn't so bad.

Hanlon, Emily. *The Swing*. Scarsdale, NY: Bradbury Press, 1979. IL: Ages 11-14.

Both 11–year-old Beth and 13–year-old Danny consider a swing to be their private refuge from problems at home. Beth, who is deaf, wishes to be more independent and resents her mother's overprotective attitude. Beth's speech sounds strange to most people, and some children make fun of her. Danny is still grieving over the death of his father several years before and resents his strict stepfather. Although Danny's stepfather appears to love him, Danny seems unable to please him and also feels he has lost his mother. When Danny lies to save face with his stepfather, Beth's freedom is affected and she thrashes out verbally at Danny. He finally confesses the truth to his stepfather. Eventually Beth and Danny begin to meet at the swing; they share their feelings and start to understand each other's problems.

Hunter, Evan. *Me and Mr. Stenner*. New York: J. B. Lippincott, 1976. IL: Ages 11-14.

Eleven–year-old Abby does not want her parents to divorce and is confused when she and her mother move into a house with Mr. Stenner. When Abby realizes Mr. Stenner is also getting a divorce so he can marry her mother, she is embarrassed about their living together and is determined not to like Mr. Stenner. Abby also resents Mr. Stenner playing father to her but eventually decides she can't help but like him a little. When both divorces are finalized and Abby's mother marries Mr. Stenner, Abby accompanies them on their honeymoon to Italy and grows very close to her stepfather. Finally Abby realizes she can love both her father and her stepfather without having to make a choice between them.

Hyde, Margaret O. *My Friend Has Four Parents*. New York: McGraw-Hill, 1981. IL: Ages 12-14.

The emotions and feelings that children bring to various family situations, including the stepfamily, are explored. Advice and ways for building self-esteem in children are covered.

Jukes, Mavis. *Like Jake and Me*. New York: Alfred A. Knopf, 1984. IL: Ages 4-6.

Alex is in awe of his strong brave stepfather but sometimes feels he may get in his stepfather's way. He is also unsure of his feelings about his mother being pregnant. Alex discovers that his stepfather has a fear of spiders when one is crawling on him. When he is able to rid his stepfather of the spider, a bond begins to form between them.

Keats, Ezra. *Louie's Search*. New York: Scholastic, 1980. IL: Ages 4-6.

When Louie searches the neighborhood for a new father, the junk man accuses him of stealing something and chases him back home. Louie's mother reassures the junk man that her son would never steal and invites him in for tea. The junk man then starts regularly visiting Louie's home. In time the junk man and Louie's mother marry.

Klass, Sheila Solomon. *To See My Mother Dance*. New York: Scribners, 1981. IL: Ages 12-14.

Jessica's father remarries, and she is determined not to accept her new stepmother. She prefers to cling to the fantasy of the mother she barely remembers. It is her stepmother who has the courage and wisdom to help Jessica deal with the reality she must now face.

Lingard, Joan. *Strangers in the House*. London: Hamish Hamilton, 1989. IL: Ages 12-14.

Stella and Calum struggle to adapt to their new life when his mother and her father re-marry and they become one family.

Mark, Jan. *Trouble Half Way*. London: Puffin, 1985. IL: Ages 8-12.

Amy's calm and settled life is suddenly shattered by events at home causing her to rethink all her quiet plans. She takes a journey on her own, encouraged by her step-father, from which she gets not just pleasure but also some confidence and affirmation.

Noble, June. *Where Do I Fit In?* New York: Holt, Rinehart, and Winston, 1981. IL: Ages 4-6.

John's mother and stepfather plan a visit to the zoo. John's mother is also expecting a new baby, and John is not sure where he fits in with his new blended family. John is assured that he is wanted and that the new baby will not take his place.

Oppenheimer, Joan L. *Gardine vs. Hanover.* New York: Crowell, 1982. IL: Ages 12-15.

Stepsisters Carolyn and Jill are antagonistic toward one another. Even their boyfriends are disturbed by their persistent hostility, which almost destroys their new stepfamily. Numerous realistic family situations are presented.

Osborne, Mary Pope. *Last One Home*. New York: Dial, 1986. IL: Ages 11-14.

A girl's father is remarrying, and she is determined not to become part of her new family. She refuses to like her stepmother and does as much as possible not to make her new family work.

Pryor, Bonnie. *Rats, Spiders, and Love*. New York: Morrow, 1986. IL: Ages 9-12.

A fifth-grader who loves the ocean is determined to keep herself and her

family in their Oregon beach home and plots to stop her mother from remarrying.

Seuling, Barbara. *What Kind of Family is This?* Racine: WI: Western
Publishing, 1985. IL: Ages 4-6.

When Jeff's mother gets remarried, he finds himself moving into a new
house with an all new family. Jeff still loves his father and doesn't really
want another father. Jeff and his stepbrother even divide their bedroom in
half but later decide to fix up the room together. Jeff finds it just takes time
to get used to his new blended family.

Shyer, Marlene Fanta. *Stepdog.* New York: Charles Scribner's Sons,
1983. IL: Ages 4-6.

Terry's stepfather decides to remarry, and Terry is determined to make his
new stepmother a part of their new blended family. His new stepmother's
dog is jealous of all the attention Terry is receiving. When the dog is ban-
ished from the house, Terry begins to empathize with the dog's problems,
and the two become friends.

Sobol, Harriet Langsam. *My Other-Mother, My Other-Father.* New
York: Macmillan, 1979. IL: Ages 7-12.

This photographic essay takes a look at the increasingly common situation
in which children must adjust to a blended family. Problems include getting
along with new stepsiblings.

Tax, Meredith. *Families.* Boston: Little, Brown, and Company, 1981. IL:
Ages 4-6.

A little girl lives with her mother most of the time but spends vacation with
her father, her stepmother, and their new baby. The girl describes the family
forms of various children she knows--an extended family, a two-parent
family, a child who's adopted, a single-father home. The girl claims the important thing in all families is how much they love each other.

Vigna, Judith. *Daddy's New Baby.* Chicago: Albert Whitman, 1982.
IL: Ages 4-6.

A small girl with divorced parents resents her father's and stepmother's new
baby. When she visits her father, the girl has to share a room with the baby
and share her father's attention as well. She helps her father prepare the
baby for an outing and saves the baby from a near disaster. Discovering that
only she can make the baby stop crying, the little girl becomes more fond of
her new stepfather.

Vigna, Judith. *She's Not My Real Mother.* Chicago: Albert Whitman, 1980. IL: Ages 4-6.

While a boy spends a weekend with his father and stepmother, he is determined not to like his new stepmother no matter how hard she tries to be friendly. His father has work to do on Sunday, so Miles must accompany his stepmother to an ice show. There he purposely gets lost to worry his stepmother. Once she finds him, his stepmother says she will not tell his father about the incident, and he decides to become her friend.

Visher, Emily B., and Visher, John S. *How to Win As a Stepfamily.* New York: Dembner, 1982. IL: Ages 16-18.

Situations and problems in Stepfamilies are covered. Although the book is written for stepparents, older stepchildren can find information in this book for dealing with the blended family.

Wolkoff, Judie. *Happily Ever after...Almost.* New York: Bradbury, 1982. IL: Ages 11-13.

This book presents remarriage and the stepfamily. The book is narrated by 11-year-old Kitty, who presents the trials and tribulations of the blended family situation.

Chapter 5

Separation And Divorce

The incidence of divorce is quite common in the western world. For example, in the United States the number of children affected by divorce each year is numbered in the millions, with approximately one out of five school-age children living in single-parent homes (Goldman & King, 1985). Most children involved in divorce are very young, averaging about 7 years of age (Beal, 1980). Wallerstein (1983) reports that marital separation and divorce are emotionally comparable to losing a parent to death. Given these findings, it is clear that family breakdown, for many children, is a traumatic and painful process.

The lives of children of separation and divorce are profoundly changed, psychologically, socially, and economically. Children must adjust to new roles and relationships as a result of family breakdown. There are often changes in the family's economic status as well as in neighborhoods, schools, and friends. These transitions have major implications for children's social and psychological functioning. Even though separation and divorce bring relief from tension and strife, for many children the breakup brings more stress, pressure, and conflicting loyalties (Kupisch, Rudolph, & Weed, 1984).

How children react to divorce is age related (Wallerstein & Kelly, 1980). For example, children who are very young at the time of divorce seem to suffer less. However, children from ages 6-8 often believe they caused the divorce. Children in the age group of 9-12 often have a difficult time with family breakdown as a result of separation and divorce. They often feel loss, rejection, shame, abandonment, and intense anger about their parents' separation.

Guidubaldi (1984) reports that most children, especially boys, going through divorce experience academic problems. Children often turn to teachers for comfort during this time. Hence, teachers must be particularly sensitive to the needs of children experiencing family breakdown.

Wallerstein (1983) notes that children of divorce must successfully resolve a number of critical "psychological tasks" in order to grow emotionally. It is critical that practitioners understand these tasks as they work with children of divorce. The following is a summary of these tasks:

1. *Achieving realistic hope regarding relationships.* Children of divorce must learn to take chances in forming relationships with others. They must keep in mind that these relationships may or may not succeed. In order for children to make an attempt at new relationships, they must be loved. Often children of divorce do not feel loved because they feel one or both of their parents have rejected them. Older children in particular may act out due to these feelings of rejection by adults. It is critical for children of divorce to realize that they can love and be loved. Furthermore, they must learn to take chances at forming new

71

relationships while knowing that some of these will be successful and others will not.

2. *Accepting the permanence of divorce.* Children of divorce often have fantasies about reuniting their parents, even though their parents may have remarried. Unlike death of a parent, when children lose a parent to divorce, the fantasy of restoring their families is strong. Practitioners must help children understand that this is not likely to happen and help them accept the permanence of divorce. Even though this may be painful for children of divorce, it is critical to them for dealing effectively with reality.

3. *Resolving anger and self-blame.* Children of divorce tend to blame their parents for being selfish and unresponsive to needs of their children. It is also common for children to blame themselves for the breakdown of their families. Children must realize that their parents are not unresponsive to their children's needs and that they must forgive their parents for divorcing. Resolving anger and self-blame is a critical task for children of divorce to accomplish.

4. *Resolving loss.* Divorce brings not only the loss of a parent but also the loss of friends and familiar surroundings. The resolution of losses associated with divorce may well be one of the most difficult tasks for children to accomplish. Since many children of divorce do not have a meaningful relationship with their absent parent, the resolution of loss becomes even more difficult. Parents and practitioners must be particular sensitive to the feelings associated with loss, and to help children express these feelings.

5. *Acknowledging the reality of the marital rupture.* Small children often experience terrifying fantasies, abandonment, and denial when their parents divorce. Since parents often experience stress during divorce, they often do not perceive problems encountered by their children. Older children are likely to suffer anxiety and even psychosomatic problems. Practitioners must help children deal with the reality of divorce through supportive counseling. Through the counseling process, children of divorce are able to resolve negative feelings about divorce and to effectively come to terms with their parent's separation.

6. *Disengaging from parental conflict and distress and resuming customary pursuits.* The resolution of this task is accomplished by children distancing themselves from the crisis in their household and resuming normal learning activities, and friendships. Parents must provide security and structure to help children keep order in their lives. If this does not occur, children may experience a significant decline in academic achievement and problems in other areas of their lives.

Finally, Wallerstein (1983) believes that children who experience separation and divorce view it as the single most important event of their childhood. Given the effects of divorce on children's lives, the following are suggestions for helping children deal with the crisis associated with divorce:

1. Regular visits with the absent parent should be arranged.
2. Talk with the child about his or her feelings related to the separation and divorce.
3. Try to keep the child's life as stable as possible through household routines, consistent discipline techniques, and school schedules.
4. Avoid giving children responsibilities beyond their age. For example, a 10-year-old should not be expected to be the chief caregiver of a younger brother or sister when the parent is absent from the house.
5. Realize that children often go through a grieving process for the parent who is absent from the home.
6. Children will sometimes blame themselves for the family breakdown, and parents must help them understand that they did not cause the separation and divorce.

The annotated books in this chapter offer a realistic picture of the kinds of problems which children of family breakdown experience. One of the critical issues covered in many of the suggested readings is that children may be relieved that the parents have finally separated; however, the love for the absent parent remains strong even if the parent treated the child poorly. None of the annotated readings present separation and divorce as a stress-free process. Most of the books present the conflicting emotions and loyalties that children of family breakdown feel.

References

Beal, E. (1980). Separation, divorce and single-parent families. In E. Carter & M. McGoldrick (Eds.), *The family life cycle*. New York: Gardner Press.

Goldman, A., & King, M. (1985). Counseling children of divorce. *School Psychology Review*, **14**, 280-290.

Guidubaldi, J. (1984). Differences in children's divorce adjustment across grade level and gender. *A report from the NASP-Kent State nation wide project*. Kent, OH: Kent State University.

Kupisch, S., Rudolph, L., & Weed, E. (1984). The impact of the divorce process in the family, March 1983, Southeastern Psychological Association. Presentation published in ERIC/CAPS. *Resources in Education*, January 1984, ed 233277.

Wallerstein, J. (1983). Children of divorce: The psychological tasks of the child. *American Journal of Orthopsychiatry*, **53**, 230-243.

Wallerstein, J., & Kelly, J. (1980). *Surviving the breakup: How children and parents cope with divorce*. New York: Basic Books.

Books on Separation and Divorce

Anderson, Penny. *A Pretty Good Team*. Chicago: Child's World, 1979. IL: Ages 6-10.

A boy named Jeff does not like to hear his parents fight, but when he learns of the divorce, he is not sure which is worse. Jeff's emotional turmoil about the divorce is emphasized throughout the story.

Angell, Judie. *What's Best For You*. New York: Bradbury, 1981. IL: Ages 11-13.

The complex and delicate relationships about divorce are explored in this book. The plot takes place in the summer months.

Berger, Fredericka. *Nuisance*. New York: Morrow, 1983. IL: Ages 10-13.

Seventh-grader Julie begins to change her image as a nuisance to her divorced parents. A neighborhood child helps her to bring about this change in herself.

Berger, Terry. *How Does it Feel When Your Parents Get Divorced?* New York: J. Messner, 1977. IL: Ages 9-14.

The emotional problems experienced by children of divorce are discussed. The problems related to family separation and lifestyle changes are covered.

Blume, Judy. *It's Not the End of the World*. New York: Bradbury, 1972. IL: Ages 10-12.

This first-person narrative is laced with humor of school and home. The child does not want her parents to divorce but deep down knows it is inevitable. The confused emotions children experience during divorce are presented.

Boeckman, Charles. *Surviving Your Parent's Divorce*. New York: Watts, 1980. IL: Ages 12-18.

The legal terms, feelings, and the adjustments that children must make when parents divorce are discussed. Strategies for dealing with the emotional and psychological problems related to divorce are emphasized.

Brown, Laurence, and Brown, Marc. *Dinosaurs Divorce: A Guide for Changing Families*. Boston: Atlantic Monthly Press, 1986; London: Collins, 1987. IL: Ages 3-8

This book gets to the heart and problems common to children during and after divorce. Advice for helping children deal with divorce is offered.

Byars, Betsy. *The Animal, the Vegetables, and John D. Jones*. New York: Delacorte, 1982. IL: Ages 10-13.

This story involves divorce and remarriage and the feelings of the children. While sharing a beach vacation, Clara and Deanie, two children of divorce, plot against John D., son of their father's girlfriend. The story ends in a near tragedy.

Carrick, Carol. *What A Wimp!* Boston: Clarion Books, 1983. IL: Ages 8-11.

A boy and his brother and their mother move to a new town after their family is broken by divorce. The children must adjust to a new school and a new neighborhood.

Cleary, Beverly. *Dear Mr. Henshaw*. New York: Morrow, 1977. IL: Ages 10-12.

This serious story is written through letters from Leigh to his favorite author. Leigh's feelings about his absent father are presented, and his world appears to be crumbling around him after the divorce of his parents.

Conrad, Pam. *Holding Me Here*. New York: Harper & Row, 1986. IL: Ages 12-15.

This story has no heroes, only victims. Robin's pain is revealed as she attempts to deal with the separation and divorce of her parents.

Danziger, Paula. *The Divorce Express*. New York: Delacorte, 1982. IL: Ages 12-13.

Phoebe struggles with the problems of joint custody and the new friends and neighborhood she must adjust to. She lives with her father during the week and with her mother on weekends.

Danziger, Paula. *It's An Aardvark-Eat-Turtle World*. New York: Delacorte, 1985. IL: Ages 11-14.

Rosie's mother is moving in with the father of Phoebe. Rosie experiences the joys of a first love, as well as the pain of racism. Rosie is the child of a

White mother and African-American father.

Duder, Tessa. *Jellybean*. London: Puffin, 1986. IL: Ages 10-13.

A modern novel about Geraldine, nicknamed Jellybean, growing up in a one-parent family.

Fine, Anne. *Goggle Eyes*. London: Puffin, 1989. IL: Ages 8-12.

Kelly Johnston is miserable because her mother is thinking of getting married. Kitty makes things more bearable when she candidly relates her experiences with "Goggle-Eyes," the man in her own mother's life.

Fisher, Lois I. *Rachel Vellars. How Could You?* New York: Dodd Mead, 1984. IL: Ages 9-12

An 11-year-old girl faces the challenges of a new school when she goes to live with her father following divorce.

Fleming, Alice. *Welcome to Grossville*. New York: Scribner's, 1985. IL: Ages 9-12.

A boy named Michael reacts to his parents' divorce. He must adjust to new friends and neighborhood.

Fox, Paula. *The Moonlight Man*. New York: Bradbury, 1986. IL: Ages 12-18.

A girl spends an unusual summer with her father, who is a writer and, as she discovers, an alcoholic. He is divorced from her mother, and the girl finds her feelings for her father are conflicting and confusing.

Gardner, Richard. *The Boys' and Girls' Book About Divorce*. New York: Science House, 1970. IL: Ages 9-12.

The text discusses the childhood fears and worries common to children of divorce. The book helps children face these problems realistically.

Gilert, Sara. *Trouble At Home*. New York: Lothrop, 1981. IL: Ages 12-18.

Family problems and crises are discussed. These include job loss, divorce, remarriage, illness and other related topics. Strategies for handling stressful situations are offered, including how to seek professional help.

Glass, Stuart. *A Divorce Dictionary: A Book For You And You Children*. Boston: Little, Brown and Company, 1980. IL: Ages 10-12.

The author is an attorney who specializes in divorce cases. The author discusses issues related to divorce, including Abandonment and Visitation Rights.

Goldman, Katie. *In The Wings*. New York: Dial, 1982. IL: Ages 12-16.

Jessie has her dream come true of being a member of the cast in a school play. The jitters of opening night are overcome by Jessie even though her parents are divorcing.

Greene, Constance. *A Girl Called Al*. New York: Viking Press, 1969.

This book is about a girl who comes from an intact family. Her best friend, Al, comes from a divorced family. Al tries to be a nonconformist to hide the hurt and loneliness.

Hallstead, William F. *Tundra*. New York: Crown, 1984. IL: Ages 10-14.

Jamie's love for a dog named Trundra helps her adjust to her parents' divorce.

Hest, Amy. *Pete and Lily*. Boston: Clarion/Houghton, 1986. IL: Ages 9-12.

Two 12-year-old girls are brought together in friendship by a common bond: both have only one parent. One girl's parents are divorced, and the other girl's father is dead.

Impey, Rose. *My Mum and Our Dad*. London: Puffin, 1990. IL: Ages 2-7.

This is the story of two families. In one a boy lives with his mother; in the other, twin girls live with their father. The book captures the conflict often found in families.

Krementz, Jill. *How It Feels When Parents Divorce*. New York: Knopf, 1984. IL: Ages 9-14.

Nineteen boys and girls, ages 8 to 16, share the experiences and feelings they had while adjusting to divorced families. The children come from a variety of backgrounds.

Leshan, Eda. *What's Going to Happen to Me? When Parents Separate or Divorce*. New York: Four Winds, 1978. IL: Ages 6-12.

This book explores the problems and feelings common to children who experience separation and divorce.

MacLachlan, Patricia. *Sarah, Plain and Tall*. London: Puffin, 1985. IL: Ages 8-12.

When Caleb and Anna's father advertises for a new wife in the newspaper, they little expect that the wonderful Sarah, plain and tall, will come into their lives.

Mann, Peggy. *My Daddy Lives in a Downtown Hotel*. Garden City, NY: Double Day, 1973. IL: Ages 9-12.

A young boy who is convinced that his parents' separation is his fault.

Mark, Jan. *The Twig Thing*. London: Viking, 1988. IL: Ages 5-8.

Two sisters and their single-parent father move into a new house. Initially apprehensive, the girls gradually become accustomed to their new home.

Mazer, Norma Fox. *A, My Name is Ami*. New York: Scholastic/Apple, 1986. IL: Ages 11-13.

This book is about two best friends, Mia and Ami. Mia helps Ami to cope with her parents' separation.

Newman, Marjorie. *Family Saturday*. London: Harmish Hamilton, 1977. IL: Ages 5-10.

This is a story about the problems that can occur when a parent remarries.

Pursell, Margaret. *A Look At Divorce*. Minneapolis: Lerner Publications, 1978. IL: Ages 5-8.

Through short text and photographs of children in loving situations with one or both parents, this book helps children understand that even though their parents will no longer stay together, they will be cared for and loved.

Richardson, Judith. *David's Landing*. Boston: Woods Hole Historical Collection, 1984. IL: Ages 9-12.

A boy who is very unhappy comes to live in a small town with his biological father. The boy is able to adjust in his new home away from his biological mother.

Sach, Elizabeth-Ann. *Shyster*. New York: Atheneum, 1985. IL: Ages 8-11.

A small girl's divorced mother wants her to spend the summer with her and her boyfriend. The girl resists the idea and would much rather be with her biological father (even though he deserted the family) than stay with her mother and the mother's boyfriend.

Smith, Miriam. *Annie and Moon*. London: Puffin, 1988. IL: Ages 3-7.

A New Zealand story about a mother and child having to find a new place to live when the father leaves. A grandma offers a solution to their problem.

Talbert, Marc. *Thin Ice*. London: Hamish Hamilton, 1986. IL: Ages 10-13.

Martin feels torn between the dependence of his diabetic sister, his busy mother and his own need for his absent father. Lonely Martin's school work suffers as do his friendships. When his mother begins to date his teacher, Martin feels his life has been completely shattered.

Townsend, John Rowe. *Rob's Place*. London: Puffin, 1988. IL: Ages 10-13.

Rob's parents are divorced and his mother remarries. His biological father lives some distance away and can only visit on Saturdays. Rob is unhappy, and is helped by his stepfather and biological parents.

Vigna, Judith. *Grandma Without Me*. Niles, IL: Whitman, 1984. IL: Ages 4-6.

Because of his parents' divorce, a boy struggles to stay in contact with his grandmother.

Voigt, Cynthia. *A Solitary Blue*. New York: Atheneum, 1983. IL: Ages 12-15.

This text offers a portrayal of fractured family relationships and of love--how it perseveres and nourishes, and how it heals the deepest wounds.

Wignell, Edel. *Marmalade, Jet and the Finnies*. London: Hamish Hamilton, 1987. IL: Ages 5-8.

It is difficult for Jessica to adjust to her new life, with her parents separated. Pets prove to be Jessica's comfort and she is helped by Mr. Chan, a teacher, and Mrs. Singh, a neighbor.

Chapter 6

Child Abuse

Child abuse is one of the major social problems nationally and internationally. In the United States alone, the research suggests that up to 340,000 children are maltreated each year (Pardeck, 1990). There is little to suggest that this trend will change in the near future.

If one uses bibliotherapy with abused children, it should be clear that the technique must be used in an appropriate fashion. It should also be recognized that many traditional therapies do not work well with the abused child. As noted by Naitove (1978), abused children frequently perceive conventional verbal methods of assessment and treatment as threatening. Often the abused child does not have the emotional and cognitive development requisite to being helped by traditional therapies. The child also has a difficult time forming relationships, particularly therapeutic ones. Abused children often have an ongoing fear of being abused and often avoid emotional contact with others. Given this situation, new and innovative approaches must be implemented to treat the abused child. Finally, it should be noted that bibliotherapy is viewed as a supportive therapy and not the therapy of choice for treating child abuse.

Much of the research on child abuse suggests that abused children often have long-term psychological and social problems as a result of maltreatment by others. Germain, Brassard, and Hart (1985) suggest that emotional symptoms such as anger, fear, denial, repression, and apathy are often a result of child abuse in children. Furthermore, a number of inappropriate behaviors including acting out, withdrawal, somatic symptoms, nightmares, and phobias are found to be indicative of abused children. At times children are referred to therapists because of problems related to their abuse. Others may be referred because they are extremely withdrawn, isolated, or have academic problems. In the course of therapy, the abuse is discovered, thus helping the therapist understand why the child is having problems in his or her social functioning.

The practitioner must realize that child abuse is part of an overall pattern of abusive behavior, the family system, as well as the personality make-up of the perpetrator. Often the reactions of the family will either enhance or interfere with social treatment. Family therapy has been found to be an extremely effective strategies for dealing with abusive families.

Interviews with abused children may be damaging if the practitioners exhibits shock or disapproval of the child, the parents, or the information that the child provides. England and Thompson (1988) argue that practitioners should tell children what will be done with the information and what to expect next.

Helpers who work with abused children should be prepared to provide support and understanding for all persons involved in the abuse. Obviously, it is natural for the therapist to feel anger at the person who abused the child. These feelings must be recognized and resolved in order for the therapist to be effective. Practitioners who are overly sympathetic with abused children may lose objectivity and the ability to help the child and his or her family.

It should always be recognized that abused children are not easy clients to treat. They have to learn to trust themselves, their environment, and the people who are attempting to help them. These children have experienced inconsistency in their environments, and physical and emotional pain. It is easier to withdraw from the world than face the emotional pain caused by the abuse. Thompson and Rudolph (1988) suggest the following considerations when doing treatment with abused children. These points will also help one to implement bibliotherapy:

1. The helping person should be prepared to become totally involved with the child in order to prove that people can be trusted, and be particularly prepared for the child to test one's caring for him or her.
2. The helper will need to be a good adult model by demonstrating consistent and positive behaviors when interacting with the child.
3. In addition to building a positive relationship between the helper and the child, attention must be given to building and enhancing the child's self-concept. The child must feel good about him or herself before effective therapy can proceed.
4. One of the most important dynamics of the relationship between the helper and the child is to allow the child to talk about the abuse in a nonthreatening environment. Bibliotherapy can be particularly helpful if the therapist is skillful at using books in treatment.

Children must be allowed to ventilate their feelings in order to resolve the issues that confront them related to the abuse. Unfortunately many abused children think they deserved the abuse. Elkind (1980) points out that young children in the age group 7-11 will say their parents are good even though they are abusive. Since they have a limited cognitive view of the world and cannot verbalize their limited understanding of the world, children believe their parents can be nothing but good. Bibliotherapy can be very useful for young children if it is combined with role playing and play therapy. With this approach, abused children can begin to express their feelings and concerns.

Finally, the books annotated in this chapter deal with the problem of child abuse in a realistic fashion. Several of the titles can be used as preventative tools because they present, among other things, appropriate and inappropriate touching by adults. Many of the emotional and behavioral problems associated with child abuse are developed in the titles that follow. Consequently, one should view these titles as tools not only for treatment but also for prevention.

References

Elkind, D. (1980). Child development and counseling. *Personnel and Guidance Journal*, **58**, 353-355.

England, L., & Thompson, C. (1988). Counseling child abuse victims: Myths and realities. *Journal of Counseling and Development*, **66**, 370-373.

Germain, R., Brassard, M., & Hart, S. (1985). Crisis intervention for maltreated children. *School Psychology Review*, **14**, 291-299.

Naitove, C. (1978). Research and special projects: Protecting our children: The fight against molestation. *Arts and Psychotherapy*, **12**, 115-116.

Pardeck, J. T. (1990). Children's literature and child abuse. *Child Welfare*, **69**, 83-88.

Thompson, C., & Rudolph, L. (1988). *Counseling children*. (2nd ed.) Pacific Grove, CA: Brooks/Cole.

Books on Child Abuse

Adler, C. S. *Fly Free*. New Jersey: Coward-McCann, 1984. IL: Ages 6-8.

Shari learns to cope with having been abused, even though her relationship with her mother is strained.

Anderson, Deborah, and Finne, Martha. *Margaret's Story*. Minneapolis: Dillion Press, 1986. IL: Ages 5-10.

Margaret must go to court because she has been sexually abused. Margaret was afraid to tell her parents, because the perpetrator told her not to tell anyone. Margaret finds out that what happened to her is against the law. This book is based on an actual case.

Anderson, Deborah, and Finne, Martha. *Michael's Story*. Minneapolis: Dillion Press, 1986. IL: Ages 5-10.

Michael's parents make him feel bad about himself. His mother tells him that he is fat and his dad calls him stupid. After a fight at school, Michael talks to a social worker. Therapy helps him deal with his sadness and anger.

Anderson, Deborah, and Finne, Martha. *Robin's Story*. Minneapolis, MN: Dillion Press, 1986. IL: Ages 5-8.

Robin's mother often gets mad and spanks him. She spanks him with a belt and cuts him with a cookie tin thrown at him. He must go to a physician because of the injury, and the past physical abuse is discovered.

Bauer, Marion. *Foster Child*. New York: Seabury, 1977. IL: Ages 11-18.

Twelve-year old Rennie must defend herself from the sexual advances made by her foster father. Feeling ashamed and confused, Rennie flees her foster home and seeks help from adults willing to assist her.

Bawden, Nina. *Squib*. New York: Lothrop, 1982. IL: Ages 10-13.

An abused child is rescued by his friends.

Byars, Betsy. *Cracker Jackson*. New York: Viking, 1984. IL: Ages 10-13.

An 11-year-year-old boy is instrumental in getting his ex-babysitter to seek shelter from her husband, who beats her and their baby.

Byars, Betsy. *The Pinballs*. New York: Harper and Row, 1977. IL: Ages 11-16.

Three foster children--two teenagers who have been physically abuse and a young boy abandoned by his mother--share a home. They share feelings about being victims of abuse and begin to feel like a family within the security of their foster home.

Coolidge, Olivia. *Come By Here*. Boston: Houghton Mifflin, 1970. IL: Ages 10-14.

A 7-year-old African American child is abused by her relatives.

Culin, Charlotte. *Cages of Glass, Flowers of Time*. New York: Bradbury, 1979. IL: Ages 12-14.

Claire, a 7-year-old child, has been reared by her father's wealthy mother. After her grandmother's death, Claire must return to her abusive mother.

Cunningham, Julia. *Come To The Edge*. New York: Avon, 1978. IL: Ages 10-13.

This story is about Grave, an unwanted, abused child.

Dahl, Roald. *Boy: Tales of Childhood*. New York: Farrar, 1984. IL: Ages 10-14.

A child is beaten at a boarding school.

Dolan, Edward. *Child Abuse*. New York: Watts, 1980. IL: Ages 12-14.

The principle areas of child abuse, including physical and sexual abuse, are outlined for the younger reader.

Fine, Anne. *Stranger Danger*. London: Hamish Hamilton, 1991. IL: Ages 5-10.

Joe learns his safety rules about speaking to strangers, but he soon realizes that rules aren't everything. One must use common sense as well.

Girard, Linda Walvoord. *My Body Is Private*. Niles, IL: Albert Whitman and Company, 1984. IL: Ages 5-10.

This book discusses appropriate and inappropriate touching of children by adults. In the language of a child, the book addresses the parts of the child's body that should or should not be touched by adults, unless there is good reason to do so. The book explains to children what they should do if an adult touches private parts of the child's body. Jon R. Conte, PhD, includes a note to parents about what they should do if a child is sexually abused, including how to contact a child protection agency.

Hamilton, Virginia. *Sweet Whispers, Brother Rush*. New York: Avon, 1982. IL: Ages 12-14

Through the ghostly intervention of a dead uncle, a young girl witnesses the past experiences of her mother, who abused her brother out of ignorance and frustration and who must now leave the children alone 6 days a week to support them as a nurse.

Haskins, James. *The Child Abuse Help Book*. Niles, IL: Albert Whitman, 1981. IL: Ages 11-14.

Child abuse is covered in this book. The problems that lead to and stem from child abuse accompany directions for help, including agencies, resource centers, and suggestions for personal action.

Holland, Ruth. *Mill Child*. New York: Macmillan, 1970. IL: Ages 11-14.

A history of child labor in factories and mines reveals the exploitation and abuse that continues today in the treatment of migrant children.

Hunt, Irene. *The Lottery Rose*. New York: Charles Scribner's, 1976. IL: Ages 5-10.

Physically abused by his alcoholic mother and her boyfriend, a 7-year-old boy has behavioral problems and becomes distrustful and isolated from others. He is reluctant to enter a boy's home, but only there does he develop a positive relationship with other adults and counselors.

Hyde, Margaret. *Cry Softly! The Story of Child Abuse*. Philadelphia: Westminster, 1980. IL: Ages 10-13.

This story offers an easy-to-read overview of historical and contemporary patterns of child abuse, with a listing of organizations for obtaining help.

Irwin, Hadley. *A Girl Like Abby*. London: Puffin, 1985. IL: Ages 11-18.

Chip falls in love with Abby when he is thirteen, but he is sixteen before he discovers what makes Abby seem so distant. Chip finds out that Abby is a victim of sexual abuse, and the perpetrator is her father. Abby finally receives help from authorities.

Kellogg, Marjorie. *Like the Lion's Tooth*. New York: Farrar, Straus, and Giroux, 1972. IL: Ages 11-14.

Eleven-year old Ben, who has been physically and sexually abused by his father, is sent to a school for "problem children." He runs away from the school in an attempt to find his mother. Ben resigns himself to his situation and begins making friends.

MacPherson, Margaret. *The Rough Road*. San Diego: Harcourt Brace Jovanovich, 1966. IL: Ages 11-14.

A child who is mistreated by his foster parents has little joy in life. He is able to improve his emotional well-being after he makes a close friendship with someone who cares.

Mazer, Harry. *The War on Villa Street*. New York: Delacort, 1978. IL: Ages 11-14.

Willis, an 8-year-old boy, is frequently beaten by his alcoholic father--once to a point near unconsciousness. After striking back at his father, Willis runs away but returns, hoping things will improve.

Moeri, Louise. *The Girl Who Lived On The Ferris Wheel*. New York: Avon, 1979. IL: Ages 10-14.

In a disturbing and suspenseful book, a girl's emotionally troubled mother beats her. The girl reports the mother to the authorities.

Newman, Susan. *Never Say Yes To A Stranger: What Every Child Should Know to Stay Safe*. New York: Putnam/Perigee, 1985. IL: Ages 4-10.

This book attempts to teach children that they should have a healthy fear of strangers and what children should do when they find themselves in trouble with a stranger.

Norris, Gunilla. *Take My Walking Slow*. New York: Atheneum, 1970. IL: Ages 10-14.

A small boy suffers at the hands of a violent alcoholic father. It is hoped that once the boy and his father move to a new home, the abuse will stop.

O'Hanlon, Jacklyn. *Fair Game*. New York: Dial Press, 1977. IL: Ages 11-18.

Fourteen-year-old Denise is in turmoil after she discovers her new stepfather watching her undress. When her stepfather makes sexual advances toward Denise's younger sister and a friend, the girls tell Denise's mother, who forces her husband to leave.

Orr, Rebecca. *Gunner's Run*. New York: Harper and Row, 1980. IL: Ages 8-11.

Frequently beaten by his alcoholic father, 9-year-old Gunner runs away from home. He is able to develop a better self-concept through his association with an elderly man who is dying.

Peterson, P. J. *Going For The Big One*. New York: Delacorte, 1986. IL: Ages 10-14 .

This story is about a group of children abandoned by their stepmother. They try to find their father, who has gone looking for work.

Piowaty, Kim. *Don't Look Into Her Eyes*. New York: Atheneum/Margaret K. McElderry. IL: Ages 10-13.

Jason is left to care for his toddler brother when their emotionally ill mother deserts them. The children finally receive help.

Rabe, Bernice. *Rass*. Wheaton, IL: Nelson, 1973. IL: Ages 11-14.

Set during the depression, this story is about a sharecropper family. The child and his rigid father have a love/hate relationship.

Roberts, Willo Davis. *Don't Hurt Laurie*. New York: Atheneum, 1978. IL: Ages 11-14.

Physically abused by her mother since the age of 3, 11-year old Laurie is afraid to approach any adult about the situation. With the aid of her concerned stepbrother, Laurie is finally able to tell her stepfather the truth, with her mother eventually receiving treatment.

Russell, Pamela, and Stone, Beth. *Do You Have A Secret?* Minneapolis: Comp-Care Publications, 1986. IL: Ages 10-14.

The text presents concepts of secrets and trust in a manner that encourages abused children to seek help.

Schlee, Ann. *Ask Me No Questions*. New York: Holt, Rinehart & Winston, 1982. IL: Ages 11-14.

This book is based on a true 19th-century British incident at an "asylum" where hundreds of children were starved and abused.

Smith, Doris. *Tough Chauncey*. New York: Morrow, 1974. IL: Ages 11-14.

A boy is caught between torrents of physical and verbal abuse from his dictatorial grandfather. The child's mother does not show him affection, and foster care finally appears to be the best placement for the boy.

Stanek, Muriel. *Don't Hurt Me, Mama*. Niles, IL: Whitman, 1983. IL: Ages 5-8.

A girl narrates the story of how her mother begins neglecting and abusing her until school officials intervene, with a connection to the community health center.

Wachter, Oralee. *Close To Home*. New York: Scholastic, 1986; London: Viking, 1986. IL: Ages 8-11.

The book addresses various child-safety issues in a nonthreatening approach. A number of abduction situations are portrayed.

Wachter, Oralee. *No More Secrets For Me*. London, Puffin, 1984. IL: Ages 10-13.

This book helps children to understand the difference between loving and touching and abusive touching. Using events known to children that include babysitters, parents, relations, friends—the book assists children through the maze of conflicting emotions related to invasion of privacy.

Wash, Jill. *A Chance Child*. New York: Avon, 1980. IL: Ages 11-14.

A small boy raised in a locked closet escapes from his prison. He wanders down a river, through a lock, and into the past, where he finds children of the Industrial Revolution just as mistreated as he.

Weik, Mary. *The Jazz Man*. New York: Aladdin, 1977. IL: Ages 8-12.

The wonderful music from a room across the court in his Harlem home alleviates the loneliness of a sickly 9-year-old boy, until his parents' absence threatens to become abandonment.

Chapter 7

Foster Care

In 1983, there were approximately 500,000 children in foster care throughout the United States (Pardeck, 1973). Only a decade earlier, there were only half this number in care. The increase of children in foster care has been attributed to the growing awareness of child abuse and neglect, as well as to the numerous problems now facing American families. Some of the critical concerns facing the foster care system are the increasing numbers of children entering the system, the tendency for children to move from foster home to foster home, and the lack of permanency felt by many foster children. Research by Hazel (1976) reports similar trends in foster care systems throughout Europe.

In the United States, efforts have been made to reduce the unnecessary placement of children in foster care. In particular, PL–96–272 (Adoption Assistance and Child Welfare Act, 1980) was passed in response to the drifting experienced by foster children and to insure that children find permanent homes. Even though the judgment is still out on PL–96–272, the law is surely in the right direction.

Within the United States, we know a great deal about the foster care system and the unique problems facing foster children. Some of these are as follows:

1. Children in foster care come from all walks of life. However, there is a tendency for children in the system to be poor and from minority families (Pardeck, 1983).
2. The average stay in the foster care system is about 3 1/2 years. Unfortunately, biological families often do not have access to quality social services while their children are in care (Pardeck, 1983).
3. Children in foster care often have parental visiting as an integral part of their treatment plans. Most judges insist on visitation between foster children and biological parents as an intricate part of treatment (Fanshel, 1976).
4. The goal is to return all foster children to their biological parents. When this is not possible, the child should be placed for adoption. Nationally there are approximately 150,000 children available for adoption (Pardeck, 1983).
5. Nearly 40% of the children in foster care are 13 years old or older (Pardeck, 1983).
6. Approximately 85% of the children in foster care have been abused or neglected (Pardeck, 1983).
7. The number of children spending their entire childhood in foster care is close to 7% (Pardeck, 1983).
8. Research reports that over 25% of children in foster care have been placed in three or more foster homes (Pardeck, 1983).

Given the limited availability of comparable data, it is hard to know whether or not the United States tends to use foster care more frequently than similar industrialized countries. The problems that plague the foster care system in the United States are apparently not unique to this country. Britain, even though it has a more developed social welfare system, faces similar problems. In 1983, the British Association of Adoption and Foster Care Agencies presented evidence on this to the House of Commons Social Services Committee. The evidence reported that "too many children may come into care unnecessarily; too many children once in care stay in care too long; too many children in care are cared for in ways which are inappropriate to their needs" (British Association for Adoption and Fostering, 1983, pp. 12-13).

Hazel (1976) notes that of the 17 different European countries studied by the Council of Europe's Coordinated Research Group, all had a developed foster care system. Hazel (1976) notes that "In all the industrialized European countries there are children who can no longer remain in their own home with their parents because society is no longer willing to tolerate their conduct or because their parents are ill, separated, have disappeared or have neglected or ill-treated their children" (p. 310).

Regardless of the country, one of the major problems facing children in foster care is that their lives have been disrupted through placement. The helping person working with children in foster care must be aware of the numerous problems related to the lack of stability in the lives of foster children. Foster children do not know how long they will be in care, and this lack of uncertainty must be dealt with by the foster parents and child welfare workers.

One of the major problems that helping adults must realize in relation to foster children is that separation from biological parents is a major crisis for these children. They must be sure that foster children know their parents will visit them regularly and that the goal is to get them back to their biological families.

Foster care also involves new roles, positions, and realignment in the foster family. These changes within the foster family must be recognized and dealt with by the foster parents and child welfare workers. Children who have been placed because of abuse or neglect may be especially troubled by the problems related to placement in care.

The annotated books listed in this chapter realistically present problems facing children placed in foster care. By reading about story characters in foster care, children are better able to cope with the foster care experience.

References

British Association for Adoption and Fostering. (1983). BAAF evidence to select committee. *Adoption and Fostering*, **7**, 11-17.

Fanshel, D. (1976). Status changes of children in foster care: Final results of the Columbia University longitudinal study. *Child Welfare*, **55**, 143–

171.

Hazel, N. (1976). Child placement policies: Some European comparisons. *Adoption and Fostering*, **6**, 315-326.

Pardeck, J. T. (1983). *The forgotten children: A study of the stability and continuity of foster care.* Washington, DC: University Press of America.

Books on Foster Care

Adler, Carole. *The Cat That Was Left Behind*. New York: Clarion, 1981. IL: Ages 10–14.

Chad Lester, a 13–year–old foster child, has been sent to another foster home. A parallel is drawn between 13–year–old Chad and a stray cat. As Chad tames the cat and cares for it, he gradually comes to terms with the facts he has long denied—that his unmarried mother who now has married does not want him back with her.

Adler, Carole. *The Magic of the Glits*. New York: Macmillan, 1979. 114 pp. IL: Ages 9–13.

Two children of misfortune, thrown together for the summer, must make the best of it. Jeremy, a 12–year–old, is recuperating from a broken leg. Lynette, a 7–year–old, is placed in Jeremy's home. Problems begin to arise between Jeremy and the foster child, Lynette; however, they are able to work them out.

Anderson, Deborah, and Finne, Martha. *Jason's Story*. Minneapolis: Dillion Press, Inc, 1986. IL: Ages 5–10.

Seven–year–old Jason lives with his biological mother. For part of his life, Jason lived with foster parents. He was placed in foster care because his mother neglected him. The story of Jason helps foster children understand why they have been placed in care and learn to deal with the emotional conflicts related to placement.

Ashley, Bernard. *The Trouble With Donovan Croft*. London: Puffin, 1977. IL: Ages 10-14.

A story about a fostered West Indian child who refuses to speak.

Bunting, Eve. *If I Asked You, Would You Stay?* New York: Lippincott, 1984. IL: Ages 12–18.

Crow has been rejected by his mother and placed in a series of foster homes. He runs away from his last foster home, not because he did not receive love and support but because he was afraid of another rejection. When Crow meets another child who has been abused, their relationship helps both children to adjust to problems they are confronted with.

Byars, Betsy. *The Pinballs*. New York: Harper and Row, 1977: London: Puffin, 1977. IL: Ages 11–18.

Fifteen–year–old Carlie, 13–year–old Harvey, and 8–year–old Thomas have been abused or neglected. The three children are placed with the Mason family. The children's reaction to placement include hostility, withdrawal, and depression. In time, the children feel more secure in the Mason's family.

Cresswell, Helen. *Dear Shrink*. London: Puffin, 1988. IL: Ages 10-13.

Oliver's parents thought they had made suitable arrangements for Oliver, William, and Lucy with Barby. Barby dies as a result of an accident and they are placed in care. Oliver enlivens life by launching into an imaginary correspondence with Jung in which all of the children's fears are brought out into the open.

Eige, Lillian. *Cady*. New York: Harper, 1987. IL: Ages 9–12.

Cady runs away from his abusive aunt. He stays a while with a cousin, but one day he is told to leave. He moves from home to home. Cady is a classic example of how foster children feel, that is, not feeling at home or safe with anyone. It is not clear what becomes of Cady's life.

Greenfield, Eloise. *Grandmama's Joy*. New York: Putnam, 1980. IL: Ages 4–9.

In infancy, Rhondy is orphaned when her parents are killed. Rhondy is placed with her grandmother, who helps her deal with the pain of losing her biological parents.

Guy, Rosa. *Edith Jackson*. London: Puffin, 1984. IL: Ages 11-18.

The story of a young black orphan, struggling against poverty and prejudice to keep together the remnants of her family,

Hahn, Mary Downing. *Daphne's Book*. New York: Clarion, 1983. IL: Ages 10–18.

Daphne and her sister Hope live with their grandmother. Their parents have died, and their grandmother is emotionally troubled. Daphne and Hope are placed in an institutional setting; they eventually are placed with a cousin.

Hall, Lynn. *Mrs. Portree's Pony*. New York: Scribner's, 1986. IL: Ages 9–12.

It has been 7 years since Addie's mother, Gloria, prevailed on her old friend, Alice, to take in her daughter because she didn't want Addie living with them anymore. Alice cannot care for her anymore, and Addie is placed in loving foster care. Addie adjusts well to her new foster home and finally forgives her mother for not caring for her.

Holz, Loretta. *Foster Child*. New York: Messner, 1984. IL: Ages 9-12.

Peter, a boy, tells his own story. His mother, abandoned by her husband, Peter's father, begins drinking heavily. No longer able to function as a parent, Peter's mother must place him in foster care.

Hyde, Margaret O. *Foster Care and Adoption*. New York: Watts, 1982. IL: Ages 13-18.

This book describes the current trends in adoption and foster care and discusses hard-to-place children, black market adoption, surrogate mothering, and the search for biological parents by adoptees. A number of case studies are presented.

King-Smith, Dick. *The Cuckoo Child*. London: Viking, 1991. IL: Ages 7-12.

A pair of geese seem perfect foster parents for Jack's ostrich egg. But what will they make of a giant son who sinks when he should swim, and runs faster than any bird on earth?

Leach, Michael. *Don't Call Me Orphan*. Philadelphia: Westminister, 1979. IL: Ages 10–14.

Kenny is 14 and lives in a children's home. He is not an orphan but has been placed in care because of his alcoholic father and divorced mother, who are irresponsible. Even though Kenny has been rejected by his biological parents, through help from the professional staff at the children's home, he is gradually able to deal with the pain of rejection.

MacLachlan, Patricia. *Mama One, Mama Two*. New York: Harper and Row, 1982. IL: Ages 4–8.

Mama One is Maudie's biological mother; Mama Two is Maudie's foster mother. Maudie is placed in foster care due to the emotional problems of her mother. Although Maudie was very depressed after placement, she begins to feel secure in her foster home and hopes to return to her biological mother.

McCutcheon, Elsie. *Storm Bird*. New York: Farrar, 1987. IL: Ages 13 –18.

Jenny's father must go to sea, so he leaves her with an aunt. Jenny's mother is dead, and Jenny has a close loving relationship with her father. Jenny experiences the loss and separation of her father throughout the story.

Mebs, Gudrun. *Sunday's Child*. New York: Dial Books, 1986. IL: Ages 7-11.

Ten-year-old Jenny finally is placed in a foster home after living in an orphanage as long as she can remember.

Myers, Walter Dean. *Won't Know Till I Get There*. New York: Viking, 1982. IL: Ages 11–15.

Fourteen–year–old Stephen, a middle–income child, matures one summer when his parents decide to foster a less fortunate child. Earl, who has experienced numerous foster placements, is suspicious when he is placed with Stephen's family. The problems of both Stephen and 13–year–old Earl are described, including the difficulty of placing Earl for adoption.

Newman, Marjorie. *Michael and the Jumble-Sale Cat*. London: Puffin, 1987. IL: Ages 5-10.

A sensitive yet realistic look at a small boy's experiences of life in a children's home.

Nixon, Joan Lowery. *Caught in the Act*. New York: Bantam, 1988. IL: Ages 11–18.

Mike has been adopted by a family of German immigrants. Mike is mistreated and moves in with a new family. The novel takes place in the mid–19 century.

Nixon, Joan Lowery. *A Family Apart*. New York: Bantam, 1987. IL: Ages 11–18.

The six Kelly children are sent West, in 1860, on a train filled with orphans to be adopted by families. The children feel abandoned by their mother, and they feel worse when they are to be separated from each other.

Paterson, Katherine. *The Great Gilly Hopkins*. New York: Thomas Y. Crowell, 1978: London: Puffin, 1978. IL: Ages 10-14

Abandoned by her mother 8 years ago, 11-year-old Gilly sets out to create trouble in her third foster home. Gilly mistreats another younger foster child and is extremely rude to her new foster parent, who is the first adult ever to really care about Gilly. When Gilly makes contact with her biological mother, she runs away but finds her mother doesn't really want her. Although Gilly finally forms an attachment to her foster mother, she must reluctantly leave to live with her grandmother.

Piepgras, Ruth. *My name is Mike Trumsky*. Chicago, IL: Child's World, 1979. IL: Ages 6–10.

Depicting the confusion foster children feel, this book shows that it is all right to love both foster parents and biological parents. The material on foster care is factual.

Rowlands, Avril. *Letty*. London: Puffin. 1984. IL: Ages 10-13.

Unwanted by her parents, Letty has spent much of her life in the children's home. She often gets in trouble and hopes for a home with a family.

Stanek, Muriel. *My Little Sister*. Chicago: Albert Whitman, 1981. IL: Ages 4–8.

An Asian child named Penny is placed in foster care. Penny is rejected by the foster parent's biological daughter. In time the biological daughter accepts Penny and is sad when she leaves to be adopted.

Wolitzer, Hilma. *Toby Lived Here*. New York: Farrar, Strauss, and Giroux, 1978. IL: Ages 11–14.

Toby, who is a 12–year–old, is placed in foster care with her younger sister, Anne. Toby feels insecure in the foster home, while Anne feels happy and secure. Eventually the girls' mother is able to care for her daughters again. Toby gradually adjusts to her foster home and even feels sad when she must return to her biological mother.

Wosmek, Frances. *A Brown Bird Singing*. New York: Lothrop, 1985. IL: Ages 9–12.

Anego is a Native American. She lives with Anglo parents who provide emotional support to her. When she is treated poorly by Anglo children, this affects her self–esteem. Her biological father returns, and she is given the choice of leaving with her father or staying in her foster home. The reader is not informed of her choice.

Chapter 8

Adoption

When children move into an adoption setting, a number of critical steps need to be considered. First, children must begin to realize that they will not return to their biological families. Even if the child has been in extended foster care, the child may continue to harbor the fantasy of returning to the biological family. Adopting parents must help the child work through this fantasy, and the fantasy will not be given up easily. Gradually, the fantasy will be abandoned by the child, resulting in the child possibly entering a stage of mourning for his or her biological parents. If this stage occurs, the child will need help in expressing anger and pain in reminiscing about the past, and must be helped to realize that he or she will not return to the bio-logical family. Open and truthful discussion of the child's past is the most effective approach, since denial and secrecy can damage the child's social functioning (Pardeck, 1990).

Another major component of the adoption process is helping the child gain self-awareness and knowledge about the past. An adopted child develops a greater sense of continuity with the past and present if he or she has knowl-edge about biological parents as well as other significant adults who shared the past. This process will help the child give up fantasies about the past and clarify the child's sense of self as a person with continuity and connected-ness to the past and the present, as the child moves into an adoptive setting.

Once the child is placed in an adoptive setting, fantasies of returning to the biological family may continue, and the need to connect to the past contin-ues to be an important psychological factor. Adoptive parents should realize that children, especially those who have been maltreated or who are older, may be fearful, angry, and anticipating one more rejection (Pardeck, 1990). Often the first week of the adoption will go smoothly, but this period of tranquillity may be artificial because the child has not yet become bonded to the adoptive family. The "honeymoon" often ends when the adoptive child begins to feel stirrings of caring and longing which bring back old emo-tional pain. The adoptive child may even fight bonding with the family be-cause he or she is frightened of another rejection by significant others. This tumultuous time can be reframed, however, as an indication that the child is beginning to care about the adoptive parents. The more the child resists bonding and attachment to the adoptive parents, the greater the temptation may be for the child wanting to become a part of the adoptive family. Such a time period is difficult for both the child and the adoptive family (Pardeck & Pardeck, 1987).

The problems that are likely to occur during the adoption process mean that parents need help and support in dealing with the complexities of this process. Much of what is taking place is beyond the control of the child. The impact of adoption of the child is strong and clearly affects the child's identity and total psychological being. Adoptive children often continue their search for biological and environmental heritage into adulthood.

Adoptive parents also find the adoption process to be stressful. Generally, the first encounter between the adoptive child and mother is a very positive experience. Smith and Sherwen's (1983) research found that for most adoptive parents, the suspense and anxiety about the adoption is followed by a sense of relief after they finally have an opportunity to meet the child. Most parents want to take the adoptive child home as soon as possible; fears that the child may be taken away from them persist until the child is finally placed in their home (Ward, 1981). Researchers report four different types of feelings common to adoptive parents when they first meet the child (Smith & Sherwen, 1983):

1. *Thrill/Joy Happiness.* The adoptive parent is filled with unqualified joy and happiness about the adoption. This is the most common response.
2. *Disappointment.* The adoptive parent finds the meeting negative and is often quite dramatic about the first encounter. This is an atypical response to the first encounter with the child.
3. *Mixture of Joy/Happiness and Fear/Anxiety.* The parent of the adoptive child is ambiguous about the first meeting with the child. The adoptive parent feels fear and insecurity at the same time; such a response is felt by many adoptive parents during their first meeting with the child.
4. *Frightened/Uneasy/Awkward/Inadequate.* Responses in this category are typical of a small number of adoptive parents. The first encounter with the child is one in which they feel uneasy, helpless, unprepared, and generally not ready to deal with the adoptive placement.

Once the child arrives at home, the parents and child begin to assess each other and seek ways to indicate that a relationship is developing. Obviously, the early part of placement is highly stressful to both the parents and child. Parents begin to realize the range of difficulties they will encounter with the child, the amount of time that it will take to work through these difficulties, and the amount of effort it will take to make the adoption work (Jewett, 1978).

Parents often fear that they do not have the ability to bond successfully with the child. It is often a struggle to establish new routines in the family and to accomplish simple family tasks. James (1980) reports that many of the tasks will become earlier as time proceeds. The child will often test the parents in order to establish limits and may even be as difficult as possible to establish what limits the family will tolerate. This struggle will end in a positive outcome if the parents are patient. The special needs child can be particularly difficult to parent during this time period. James (1980) concludes:

New parents are often eager to do the kinds of things they enjoy doing with the child and which no doubt would also be fun for the child. It may be wiser to hold back and try first of all to establish a more ordinary family routine rather than embark upon a series of outings and treats which, while seeming to help the placement along, in reality may be creating unrealistic expectations in not promoting a natural support and communication between the child and his parents. (p. 189)

At some point the adoptive parents must understand that the reality of day-to-day family life must be played out with the child. The parents must understand the reality of the adoption process, including the strengths and weaknesses of the child. Schneider & Rimmer (1984) note that if the adoptive child is disabled, the adoptive parents—like biological parents—will mourn for the child they hoped to have but did not receive.

Finally, adoption as a core child welfare service is found in all developed countries. The problems of adoptive children and parents are similar across cultures. The shortage of children available for adoption is even greater in Europe than in the United States (Sveriges Officiella Statistik, 1976). Due to this shortage of available children, many developed countries adopt children from developing countries. This situation presents a whole new set of issues related to the phenomenon of the cross-cultural adoption. The children's books annotated in this chapter present the unique problems faced by adoptive children and their parents; a number of the books focus on the issues of cross-cultural adoptions.

References

James, M. (1980). Home-finding for children with special needs. In J. Triseliotis (Ed.), *New developments in foster care and adoption* (pp. 178-195). Boston, Mass: Routledge and Kegan Paul.

Jewett, C. (1978). *Adopting the older child.* Boston, Mass: Harvard Common Press.

Pardeck, J. T. (1990). Children's literature and foster care. *Family Therapy,* **17**, 61–65.

Pardeck, J. T., & Pardeck, J. A. (1987). Bibliotherapy for children in foster care and adoption. *Child Welfare,* **66**, 269-277.

Schneider, S., & Rimmer, E. (1984). Adoptive parents' hostility toward their adopted children. *Children and Youth Services Review,* **6**, 345-352.

Smith, D., & Sherwen, L. (1983). *Mothers and Their Adopted Children: The Bonding Process.* New York: Tiresias Press.

Sveriges Officiella Statistik. (1976). *Social Varden, 1975.* Stockholm: Statistiska Centralbyran.

Ward, M. (1981). Parent bonding in older-child adoptions. *Child Welfare*, **48**, 24-34.

Books on Adoption

Althea. *Jane is Adopted*. London: Souvenir, 1980. IL: Ages 5-8.

When Jane asks once again what adoption means, her mother tells her in a loving fashion. Her mother describes the homestudy process, the home preparations and the announcement of the placement. The mother concludes by telling Jane that adopted means belonging to a family and how happy she and her father were to adopt Jane.

Anderson, C. W. *Lonesome Little Colt*. New York: Macmillan, 1974. IL: Ages 5–8.

After a colt's mother dies, he is lonely and frightened. His colt friends all have mothers they can run to. A new mare brought to the farm adopts the little colt.

Bates, Betty. *It Must've Been the Fish Sticks*. New York: Holiday House, 1982. IL: Ages 10-13.

Brian discovers that his biological mother is alive. Brian confronts his parents and is eventually taken to Ohio to visit his biological mother. This book focuses on conflicting loyalties.

Bawden, Nina. *Familiar Passions*. London: Macmillan, 1979. IL: Ages 15-18.

The main character, Bridie, an adult who is trying to come to terms with her adoption, searches for her birthmother. Bridie discovers that her birthmother is a friend of her adoptive parents and further learns that her adoptive father is also her birthfather. After making this discovery, Bridie goes on with her life.

Bawden, Nina. *The Finding*. New York: Lothrop, 1985. IL: Ages 9–12.

Alex is placed in an adoptive family. Alex feels loved and secure in his family but runs off because of a crisis. The crisis ends, and Alex returns to his adoptive family.

Bawden, Nina. *Princess Alice*. London: A. Deutsch, 1985. IL: Ages 5-8.

Tidy Alice is transracially adopted from Africa to England. She lives in a large interracial family where she does not fit well. Alice changes her mind about her new family and adjusts to living in her new home.

Bishop, Sheila. *A Speaking Likeness*. London: Hurst and Blackett, 1976. IL: Ages 15-18.

After the death of her husband, Diana is concerned about her future and that of her daughter. Diana meets an ill young girl who is pregnant. After the child is born, the young girl wants nothing to do with her child. Diana plans to adopt the child, however, she discovers who the child's father is while on holiday.

Bloomquist, Geraldine M., and Bloomquist, Paul B. *Zachary's New Home*. New York: Magination Press, 1990. IL: Ages 3-8.

This book is written for children entering adoption or foster care. The book deals with feelings through animal characters.

Blume, Judy. *Just as Long as We're Together*. New York: Orchard, 1987. IL: Ages 11-18.

Three preadolescent girls face problems related to friendship, growing up, parents separating, fears of nuclear war, and placement for adoption. One of the girls, Alison, is a Korean girl who has been adopted. Alison's adoptive family is expecting a baby, and Alison is afraid her family won't want her anymore because she is adopted.

Bowe–Gutman, Sonina. *Teen Pregnancy*. Minneapolis: Lerner, 1987. IL: Ages 12–18.

This book is written for three groups of children: teenagers who are pregnant and looking for information and advice; sexually active teenagers concerned about pregnancy; and teenagers who feel they are not ready for sex but need reassurance. The book explains to teenagers how to avoid pregnancy and the options if one becomes pregnant, including placing the child for adoption.

Brodzinsky, Anne. *The Mulberry Bird: A Story of an Adoption*. Indianapolis, IN: Perspective Press, 1986. IL: Ages 5–10.

A young mother bird struggles to provide food and security for her newly hatched baby. After some hardships, the mother bird finds she cannot adequately care for her young one. She makes the difficult decision to let two birds who can provide a stable home adopt her baby bird.

Brown, Christine. *Goodbye Patrick*. London: Arlington Books, 1973. IL: Ages 15-18.

The Brown family decides to adopt a child. Set in Scotland, the Browns approach a Catholic child welfare agency and are approved to adopt Michael who is seven days old. In due course the Browns adopt four more children including Kim who has Indian and Chinese ancestry.

Bulla, Clyde. *Open the Door and See All the People*. New York: Crowell, 1972. IL: Ages 7–10.

Sisters Jo Ann and Teeny and their widowed mother move to a city after a fire destroys their farm. The girls miss their mother, who goes to work, but they also long for their dolls lost in the fire. Jo Ann and Teeny discover a toy–lending library, where they can borrow dolls and adopt them after proving they will care for them.

Bunin, Catherine & Bunin, Sherry. *Is That Your Sister?* New York: Pantheon, 1976. IL: Ages 5–8.

Six–year-old Catherine and her mother explain how children like Catherine and her younger sister live in foster homes until an adoptive family is found. The social worker's visit and the adoptive parents' going to court to obtain legal adoption are described. Catherine says that she and her sister don't think a lot about being adopted but just concentrate on all being a family.

Burgess, Linda Cannon. *The Art of Adoption*. New York: Norton, 1981. IL: Ages 16-18.

This text is written specifically for the adoptee, birth parents, adoptive parents, and perspective adoptive parents. Examples used to address the many relevant factors surrounding adoption include birth parents, genetic concerns, feelings of children and adolescents, the social agency's role, and sealed records.

Byrd, Elizabeth. *The Search for Maggie Hare*. London, Macmillan, 1976. IL: Ages 15-18.

A nineteen-year-old girl, Dorothea, attempts to find her birthparents. Her birthmother is a prostitute and her birthfather a murderer. She locates her birthparents, then goes on with her life. The story is set in Victorian England.

Caines, Jeanette. *Abby*. New York: Harper and Row, 1973. IL: Ages 3–8.

Young Abby delights in her mother retelling about her arrival in their home when she was less than 1 year old. Abby's many questions are answered naturally and gently. Her family is black and includes an older sibling who sometimes teases her.

Cassedy, Sylvia. *Behind the Attic Wall.* New York: Crowell, 1983. IL: Ages 12–18.

Maggie is shuffled around from place to place and is finally settled with two great–aunts. She is treated poorly by the aunts and has trouble coping with her environment. Maggie is placed in a loving family that meets her needs.

Cohen, Shari. *Coping With Being Adopted*. New York: Rosen, 1988. IL: Ages 11–15.

The common problems associated with being adopted are discussed, and ways for coping with adoption are offered. There are sections on transracial and handicapped adoptees as well as other issues related to the complexity of the adoption process.

Cray, Dorothy. *Escape From Yesterday*. London: Collins, 1970. IL: Ages 15-18.

Set in England, Fenella agrees to watch over her adopted eight-year-old niece, Belinda, while her parents travel to the United States. Fenella discovers that Belinda is extremely sensitive about being an adopted child. Belinda realizes that she is wanted and loved by her adoptive parents.

Drescher, Joan. *Your Family, My Family.* New York: Walker and Company, 1980. IL: Ages 4–8.

Various family forms are described: a two–parent family where both parents work, an adopted child's family, a family where child custody is shared by parents, and a foster family. The strengths of family life such as having a sense of belonging, sharing with others, and cooperating are emphasized.

DuPrau, Jeanne. *Adoption: The Facts, Feelings, and Issues of a Double Heritage*. New York: Messner, 1981. IL: Ages 12–17.

This book presents an overview of the emotional, ethical, and legal questions related to adoption. The book answers many of the complex questions related to the adoption process and includes a focused look at the controversy over birth-history disclosure.

Eber, Christine. *Just Momma and Me*. Chapel Hill, NC: Lollipop Power, 1975. IL: Ages 4–8.

Regina is adopted by Momma, a single parent. Later they are joined by a man named Karl, and Regina has to share her Momma. Momma and Karl eventually have a new baby, making Regina's family even larger.

First, Julia. *I Rebekah, Take You, the Lawrences*. New York: Watts, 1981. IL: Ages 8–12.

After a series of short–term foster care placements, 12–year–old Rebekah is adopted by a warm and welcoming childless couple. She has mixed feelings about leaving the orphanage, fantasies about her biological parents, and feels shame at being adopted. Rebekah yearns to love and be loved, which happens gradually when a brother is adopted into the family as well.

Fisher, Iris L. *Katie–Bo: An Adoption Story*. New York: Adama, 1987. IL: Ages 5–9.

This book is about a Korean adopted child. The book presents the emotions of biological children, including generosity and hostility, toward an adopted child.

Freudberg, Judy, & Geiss, Tony. *Susan and Gordon Adopt a Baby*. New York: Random/Children's Television Workshop, 1986. IL: Ages 3–7.

This book tells how Susan and Gordon become parents of Miles by adopting him. The story emphasizes that now they will be Miles's parents forever, and that when someone new enters the family the love just grows and grows.

Girard, Linda Walvoord. *Adoption Is For Always*. Niles, IL: Whitman, 1986. IL: Ages 4–8.

A small girl realizes she has been adopted and reacts with anger. She goes through various stages including grief, pain, loneliness, fear, curiosity about her biological parents, self–doubt, and finally, acceptance. Her adoptive parents give her support, love, and understanding. They assure her that they will always be her parents.

Gordon, Shirley. *The Boy Who Wanted a Family*. New York: Harper and Row, 1980. IL: Ages 6–9.

After years of being in a number of foster placements, 7–year–old Michael is about to be adopted. The proceedings take a full year, during which Michael feels tense about his adoption by a single woman. However, Michael adjusts well to his adoptive home.

Greenberg. Judith E., & Carey, Helen H. *Adopted*. New York: Watts, 1987. IL: Ages 5–9.

Sarah and Ryan are adopted siblings. The children also have friends who are adopted. The book includes photos of the children.

Hutton, Malcolm. *Tara*. London: Hale, 1984. IL: Ages 15-18.

An eighteen-year-old child named Tara searches for her past. Finding little comfort or information from her adoptive family, Tara leaves home at age eighteen to search for her birthparents. She discovers her birthmother is really her aunt who was killed during World War II. Tara confides in her grandmother to find out the details about her past.

Hyde, Margaret. *Foster Care and Adoption*. New York: Watts, 1982. IL: Ages 13–18.

This book describes the current trends in adoption and foster care. The author also discusses hard–to–place children, black market adoption, surrogate mothering, and the search for biological parents by adoptees. A number of case studies are presented.

Koehler, Phoebe. *The Day We Met You*. New York: Bradbury Press, 1990. IL: Ages 2-5.

This is a story about parents who adopt a young child. A mother and father talk about their joy and the excitement of preparing for the arrival of an adopted child.

Kornitzer, Margaret. *The Hollywell Family*. London: Bodley Head, 1973. IL: Ages 5-8

The Hollywells are happy with their first child, Mary, and decide to have another child. A doctor tells them that they cannot have another baby, so they decide to adopt a baby boy. The Hollywells gradually adopt a new baby named George.

Korschunow, Irina. *The Foundling Fox*. New York: Harper and Row, 1982. IL: Ages 5–8.

This is a story about a fox whose mother is killed by hunters. The fox is adopted by a vixen and her family.

Krementz, Jill. *How it Feels to be Adopted*. New York: Alfred A. Knopf, 1982. IL: Ages 8–18.

Nineteen adopted children between the ages of 8 and 16 tell their stories and share their feelings. The children represent many adoptive situations: they are from varied ethnic backgrounds; some were adopted by single parents; some have handicapped siblings; and a few of the older children are involved in searches for their biological parents. All stress the special aspects of adoption.

Lapsley, Susan. *I Am Adopted*. New York: Bradbury Press, 1975. IL: Ages 2–5.

Charles is a happy child who knows he is adopted. He is a secure and busy preschooler. Charles knows that adoption means he will have a permanent family.

Lindsay, Jeanne Warren. *Open Adoption*. Buena Park, CA: Morning Glory, 1987. IL: Ages 14–18.

This book explores the current outlook on adoption. The focus is on pregnant teenage parents and their parents. Vignettes of various cases are presented concerning pregnant teenagers. The chapters look at closed adoption, open adoption, the respective rights of birth parents and adoptive parents.

Lindsay, Jeanne Warren. *Pregnant Too Soon: Adoption Is An Option*. Buena Park, CA: Morning Glory, 1988. IL: Ages 13–18.

This book is for pregnant teenagers who must make decisions concerning their pregnancies. Adoption is presented as an alternative for the teenage parent.

Lively, Penelope. *Boy Without a Name*. London: Heinemann, 1975. IL: Ages: 9-12.

Set in England in the 1600s when Charles Stuart was king, this book is about an orphan child. When the miller to whom he was apprenticed dies, the child travels to his mother's town of birth. A priest in the town gives him a first name, Thomas. Even though adoption is not mentioned in the book, the hardships of a child without parents comes through in the story.

Livingston, Carole. *Why Was I Adopted?* Seacaucus, NJ: Lyle Stuart, 1978. IL: Ages 6–10.

A variety of issues are addressed here, including reasons biological parents give up their children, how an adoption happens, and why. The fact that the adopted child is a unique and special person is stressed.

Mayhar, Ardath. *Carrots and Miggle*. New York: Atheneum, 1986. IL: Ages 10-18.

An orphaned child moves in with relatives. The child has difficulty adjusting to a new family. Even though the child has an opportunity to move to a different new family, she decides to stay with her present one.

McDonald, Joyce. *Mail–Order Kid*. New York: Putnam, 1988. IL: Ages 9–12.

Flip receives a live fox that he ordered through the mail without telling his parents. Flip's parents have adopted Todd, a 6–year–old Korean child, who Flip feels is similar to his adoptive brother. Flip must release the fox to the wild, and through this process Flip begins to understand the benefits and pain of Todd's adoption.

McHugh, Elisabet. *Karen and Vicki*. New York: Greenwillow, 1984. IL: Ages 10–12.

Karen and her sister Meghan, both adopted Korean children, must adjust to their mother's marriage to a man with three children. The adjustment doesn't come easy for the family.

McHugh, Elisabet. *Karen's Sister*. New York: Morrow, 1983. IL: Ages 11–13.

Karen reacts to her newly adopted Korean sister and to the news of her mother's engagement to a man with three children.

Meredith, Judith. *An Now We Are a Family*. Boston: Beacon Press, 1971. IL: Ages 8–18.

How babies are adopted, why parents adopt, and why biological parents must sometimes place their children in adoption are explained. Complex issues such as illegitimacy are discussed, and a text is included for adults.

Miles, Miska. *Aaron's Door*. Boston: MA: Little, Brown, and Company, 1977. IL: Ages 5–9.

After being deserted by their biological parents, Aaron and his younger sister are sent to an adoptive home. Aaron locks a door against the world, angry and envious of his younger sister's acceptance of their new adoptive home. Gradually, the powerful but gentle love of his adoptive parents shatters Aaron's self-imposed isolation.

Milgram, Mary. *Brothers Are All the Same*. New York: Dutton, 1978. IL: Ages 4–8.

There is no difference between an adopted brother and a biological one, according to Kim and Nina.

Mills, Claudia. *Boardwalk With Hotel*. New York: Macmillan, 1985. IL: Ages 9–12.

Jessica finds out that she was adopted because her parents thought they could not have children. After she is adopted, her parents have biological children. Jessica feels she is second–best to her siblings and is convinced that she is loved less than they are by her adoptive parents. She gradually comes to terms with her feelings about her adoptive family.

Nerlove, Evelyn. *Who is David? A Story of an Adopted Adolescent and His Friends*. New York: Child Welfare League of America, 1985. IL: Ages 12-14.

A child begins to question his adoption. The parents try to provide him with answers and they finally decide to send him to an adoption support group. David meets other adopted teens and is relieved to learn they share similar fears, anger and anxieties. David, on his eighteenth birthday, meets his biological birthmother. He learns of his past and is able to reconcile his adoption.

Nickman, Steven. *The Adoption Experience: Stories and Commentaries*. New York: Messner, 1985. IL: Ages 11–18.

A child psychiatrist who treats adoptive children presents commentaries on adoption. Included are stories about children in foster care and adoption, including the problems they face. Seven different stories on adoption are presented.

Packer, Joy Petersen.*Veronica*. London: Eyre and Spottiswoode, 1970. IL: Ages 15-18.

Set in South Africa, this is a novel about Veronica who is black. She has a relationship with a British businessman and a child is born from the relationship. The child is secretly adopted by a white family. The story illuminates the racial problems in South Africa.

Plumenz, Jacqueline Horner. *Successful Adoption: A Guide to Finding a Child and Raising a Family*. New York: Crown, 1982. IL: Ages 15-18.

Information on independent adoptions, adoptions through state and private agencies, and foreign adoptions is provided. Suggestions on explaining adoption to children and answering their questions about biological parents are offered.

Pursell, Margaret. *A Look at Adoption*. Minneapolis, MN: Lerner, 1977. IL: Ages 8–18.

Questions frequently asked by children about adoption are answered. Photographs concerning adoption are included.

Roberts, Willo Davis. *Eddie and the Fairy Godpuppy*. New York: Atheneum, 1984. IL: Ages 8–10.

Eddie is convinced that he is unlovable and is destined to spend the rest of his life in the orphanage. When a cute puppy arrives, seemingly out of nowhere, Eddie believes that it is his fairy godpuppy. Children will identify with Eddie's longing to be wanted by a family.

Rosenberg, Maxine B. *Being Adopted*. New York: Lothrop, 1984. IL: Ages 7–11.

This book emphasizes the unique problems found in transracial and transcultural adoptions. Included are a 7–year–old of multiracial parents, a 10–year–old from India, and an 8–year–old Korean.

Scott, Elaine. *Adoption*. New York: Watts, 1980. IL: Ages 10–12.

This look at the adoption process explains the role of the court and social services. An analysis of the influence of the biological parents and adoptive parents on the child's personality is overviewed.

Silman, Roberta. *Somebody Else's Child*. New York: Warne, Frederick, and Company, 1976. IL: Ages 7–10.

A boy and his school bus driver learn about the love between parents and their adopted children.

Simon, Norma. *All Kinds of Families*. Chicago: Albert Whitman, 1975. IL: Ages 4–7.

Different patterns of family life are explored, including the family with adoptive children. The common factor all families share is caring for one another.

Sobol, Harriet Langsam. *We Don't Look like Mom and Dad*. New York: Coward, 1984. IL: Ages 5–10.

A photo-essay on the lives of an American couple and their two Korean sons. The concerns of the children regarding their biological parents and ethnic heritage are presented. The family unit is depicted as having love, respect, and pride.

Stein, Sara. *The Adopted One: An Open Family Book For Parents and Children Together*. New York: Walker and Company, 1979. IL: Ages 5–9.

Four–year–old Joshua feels left out when his cousins discuss their births. Joshua's adoptive mother answers his questions honestly and to the best of her ability. An adult text focuses on special problems of adopted children and the strategies one can use to encourage discussion of feelings.

Storr, Catherine. *Vicki*. London: Faber Company, 1981. IL: Ages 11-13.

Vicki, an adopted child, wonders about her biological parents. She searches for her biological parents, and this process results in changes about herself.

Tax, Meredith. *Families*. Little, Brown, and Company, 1981. IL: Ages 4–8.

Six–year–old Angie describes her own family, which includes a stepparent. She also tells about the family forms of various children she knows: a two–parent family, an adoptive family, and a single-parent family, as well as other family forms. Angie claims the important thing in all families is for members to love each other.

Wagstaff, Sue. *Wayne is Adopted*. London: A. & C. Black, 1981. IL: Ages 5-8.

Wayne, a biracial child, was adopted by the King family when he was eight. The King family has four other children, including Emma, a biracial child adopted as an infant. The Kings' lifestyle is portrayed with the children having chores, family vacations, birthdays, and school sports. The family encourages Wayne and Emma to learn about their past and their mixed heritage.

Yolen, Jane. *Children of the Wolf*. New York: Viking Kestrel, 1984. IL: Ages 10–18.

This book is based on the feral children discovered in India in the 1920s. The story is complex and tragic. The problems of the feral children after being placed in an orphanage are discussed. The children never do rejoin human society.

Chapter 9

Childhood Fears

Children's literature has been widely used as a rich resource for helping children understand and cope with fear (Tremewan & Strongman, 1991). Fiction provides children with an essentially safe environment where otherwise bewildering or alarming experiences may be structured and explained (Chambers, 1985). Since younger children versus older children report more intense and greater number of fears, bibliotherapy is particularly useful for young children (Bauer, 1980).

One of the most important emotions that children have to cope with is fear. All children have fears that appear to be related to the developmental process. As children grow older, they have a tendency to learn to avoid those situations that are likely to stimulate fear responses. Furthermore, as children grow older they develop the cognitive and emotional skills to deal more effectively with fear. For example, small children often have a fear of loud noises, the dark, and at times strangers. As children mature, they gradually learn to cope with these kinds of fears. However, if parents or other adults do not support children as they learn to deal with these kinds of fears, they may cause problems in later development. It should also be noted that fears stem directly from developmental conflicts which children may be struggling with, such as dependency and autonomy conflicts. In due course most children resolve these kinds of fears.

Fear is a powerful emotion that individuals must deal with throughout the life cycle. It is an emotion that we try to minimize or avoid. One must note that fear is a normal response for children and is an intricate part of their developmental process. As parents and helping people realize, fears in children can occur at anytime, often without warning. A child, for example, may suddenly have a fear of taking baths. The child may tell the parent that he or she is afraid of disappearing down the bathtub drain. Even though the child could not possibly fit in the drain, and the parent reassures the child such an event is not possible, the fear is still very real to the child. An excellent strategy to deal with such fear is to help the child confront it in a supportive fashion. Using force or ridicule may have a very negative impact, and ignoring the fear until it goes away may also not be effective. In terms of the fear of the bathtub drain, the parent may wish to use a doll or toy to illustrate to the child that even small things do not fit in the drain and that the child is much larger than a doll or toy. It should be understood that fears are a normal part of development and should be confronted and openly dealt with by both the child and adult.

Age is a critical variable for determining fear responses. In babies, a response to fear is one of helplessness. As parents well know, the typical response is crying. As children grow older, they may deal with fear by hiding their face in a pillow or simply running from the object causing fear. Running to the parent or hiding behind the parent is a normal response for small children dealing with fear.

Children, as they grow older, develop more sophisticated responses to fear. That is, as the child enters early adolescence, he or she may use defense mechanisms to reduce anxiety related to fear. Pardeck & Pardeck (1986, p. 72) list the major defense mechanisms for dealing with fear as follows:

1. *Withdrawal.* This is a common response in children. It is a very direct defense mechanism, in that the child simply runs from the fear through withdrawal.
2. *Denial.* This is the refusal to admit that a situation or event ever occurred. Children, for example, may react to the death of a pet by pretending the pet is still living in the house. Such an approach helps the child deal with pain on a temporary basis.
3. *Projection.* This defense mechanism involves distortion of reality. Children, like adults, often attribute their undesirable thoughts or actions to someone or something else. This can be a person or even a stuffed animal or pet. As with most defense mechanisms, the child often is not aware of when he or she is using projection. If the reality of the child becomes too distorted because of projection, the child may need clinical help.
4. *Regression.* This is an extreme form of denial in which the child completely erases a frightening event or situation from his or her consciousness. The child may literally not know the event or situation ever occurred.

All normal children and adults use defense mechanisms to cope with fear. It is not unusual for individuals to use many of these mechanisms simultaneously. They become dysfunctional when they are used to the extreme. We often learn which defense mechanisms work best for us. It is not unusual for children to learn defense mechanisms through observation of parents. Thus whole families may use very similar techniques for dealing with fear.

Parents must be aware that they play a vital role in creating fears in children. Caplan and Caplan (1983) conclude the following behaviors may well increase fear in children:

1. *Fear as a method of discipline.* When parents use fear as a method of discipline, they create unnatural dread of persons, things, or occurrences.
2. *Severe punishment.* Children tend to harbor intense anger and a wish for revenge when parents use harsh punishments and threats as a part of discipline.
3. *Excessive expectations.* Children may develop fear of failure if parents expect too much from them. The children may refuse to climb to the top of a jungle gym or ride a bike if they fear that their levels of accomplishment may not meet the standards of their parents.
4. *Overprotectiveness.* Children may develop fear if they are overly de-

pendent upon parents. If a parent does not allow a child to explore his or her environment, the child may not develop confidence to overcome fears and mastery of the environment.

5. *Overpermissiveness*. When parents do not place limits on their children, children may not learn how to control their wishes and desires. Such a situation may cause children to feel out of control, which increases their fears.

A number of activities can be used to decrease fear in children. According to Caplan and Caplan (1983) these include:

1. *Explaining the situation*. Parents must explain situations to children that may be frightening. For example, if a child is exposed to a dog for the first time, the parent must help the child understand the appropriate response to an animal that he or she has seen for the first time.
2. *Setting an example of calmness*. When natural and foreseen events occur, the parent should reassure the child that nothing is wrong. For example, when the parent and child see lightning, the parent should smile and wait for the thunder to follow.
3. *Encouraging talk about the child's feelings*. The parent should let the child know that fears are natural and that everyone is afraid of something at some time. Parents should help the child sort out imagined and real fears. For example, if a small child thinks there is a monster in the closet, the parent must show the child a monster is not there instead of telling the child that the parent will drive the monster away.
4. *Trying to effect "positive reconditioning."* Parents can replace the feared stimulus with an attractive one. An example might be when a child pets a friendly animal, the parents praises him or her for doing so.
5. *Limiting exposure that can cause fear or threatened danger*. Children should not be exposed to violence. This means making sure children do not see violent movies or television.

Finally, parents and other helpers should realize that all of us have fears at times as well as anxiety. It must be remembered that children particularly have limited understanding of fear, that their imagination is extremely vivid, and that they have a tendency to distort and magnify things that are not real. The books annotated in this chapter deal with the numerous fears that young and older children must deal with. The books that follow deal with such topics as fear of the dark, dealing with unwanted emotions, coping with the fear of failure, and understanding fear related to physical and emotional development.

References

Bauer, D. (1980). Children's fears in developmental perspectives. In L. Hersov & I. Berg (Eds.), *Out of school: Modern perspectives in truancy and school refusal* (pp. 189-208). Chichester: John Wiley and Sons.

Caplan, T., & Caplan, F. (1983). *The Early Years.* New York: Bantam/ Books.

Chambers, A. (1985). *Booktalk: Occasional writing on literature and children.* London: The Bodley Head.

Pardeck, J. A., & Pardeck, J. T. (1986). *Books for early childhood: A developmental perspective.* Westport, CT: Greenwood Press.

Tremewan, T., & Strongman, K. (1991). Coping with fear in early childhood: Comparing fiction with reality. *Early Child Development and Care,* **71**, 13-34.

Books on Childhood Fears

Adams, Edith. *The Scaredy Book*. New York: Random House, 1983. IL: Ages 4-6.

This book is about Worried Walrus. Walrus decides to spend the night with a friend. When the children go to bed, Walrus thinks he sees creatures coming through the open window, thinks he sees a snake and tiger in the dark, and hears scary noises outside the window. His friend assures Walrus that he is only looking at shadows made by clothing and the noise outside is only rain. Walrus relaxes with a nightlight on and finally goes to sleep.

Akinyemi, Rowena. *Hamster Weekend*. London: Hamish Hamilton, 1991. IL: Ages 5-8.

Tolu is anxious about starting her new school; everything is so different in Britain. After a weekend of taking care of the school hamsters, she has plenty of funny stories to tell her classmates.

Asch, Frank. *Milk and Cookies*. New York: Parents Magazine Press, 1982. IL: Ages 2-6.

Baby Bear spends the night with his grandparents. Baby Bear wakes up in the middle of the night and thinks he sees his grandfather feeding a dragon. He then has scary dreams about the dragon. After awakening, Baby Bear discovers that the dragon was really the grandfather putting wood in a glowing stove.

Barsuhn, Rochelle. *Feeling Afraid*. Chicago: Children's Press, 1982. IL: Ages 4-6.

Common fears such as being afraid of the dark and of animals are described. Also discussed is the fear of making friends, reciting in front of class, and learning new skills. The book teaches children how to overcome these fears.

Berenstain, Stan, and, Berenstain, Jan. *The Berenstain Bears in The Dark*. New York: Random House, 1982. IL: Ages 4-6.

Brother Bear reads part of a scary mystery book to his Sister. The book is scary, and Sister is not able to sleep. Papa and Mama Bear try to reassure Sister that she has nothing to fear; however, they find that a nightlight for Sister is the thing that eases her fear.

Bonsall, Crosby. *Who's Afraid of The Dark?* New York: Harper and Row, 1980. IL: Ages 2-6.

A boy claims his dog is afraid of the dark and asks a friend for advice. Suspecting that the little boy is projecting his own fears, the friend suggests that the boy should hug and sleep with the dog that night. The friend's advice seems to solve the little boy's problems.

Chevalier, Christa. *Spence and The Sleepytime Monster*. Niles, IL: Albert Whitman and Company, 1984. IL: Ages 2-6.

A boy claims there is a monster in his bedroom. He gets his mother to agree that if he sees the monster she will come to his rescue. The mother is called to the boy's room and discovers the monster is a cat.

Chorao, Kay. *Lemon Moon*. New York: Holiday House, 1983. IL: Ages 4-6.

A child tries to convince his grandparent that the patchwork in his quilt comes to life when it is dark. The Grandparent shows interest in his tale about the patchwork. While he is trying to fall asleep, the child's fantasy re-occurs; he grabs the string on the moon balloon coming from the quilt and floats into his grandparent's room to take her for a ride.

Christelow, Eileen. *Henry and The Dragon*. New York: Clarion Books, 1984. IL: Ages 4-6.

Henry Rabbit listens to a bedtime story about a dragon. He is convinced that he sees a dragon shadow on his dark wall and hears dragon noises outside his bedroom. The parents try to convince the child that the dragon is in his imagination. When the child thinks he hears the dragon outside his widow the following night, his father searches for the dragon, only to be caught in a trap devised by the child. The child discovers that his very own baseball cap is producing the scary shadow.

Corey, Dorothy. *You Go Away*. Chicago: Whitman, 1976. IL: Ages 2-6.

This book is about helping very small children deal with separation from parents. Examples of separation include parents being away from children overnight and children's first day at school.

Crowe, Robert. *Tyler Toad and The Thunder*. New York: E. P. Dutton, 1980. IL: Ages 4-6.

Tyler Toad jumps into his hole at the first sign of thunder. Various friends try to assure him that he has nothing to be afraid of. They tell Tyler that the Thunder is like a noisy parade in the skies. However, when an extra loud clap of thunder is heard, Tyler once again jumps to safety, only to find all his friends in his hiding hole.

Daly, Niki. *Joseph's Other Red Sock*. New York: Atheneum, 1982. IL: Ages 4-6

Joseph finds he has one red sock missing. With the help of his cat and some stuffed animals, he searches his room and pulls a monstrous looking mound of clothes out of his cupboard. Only after Joseph grabs at the monster and chases it back into the cupboard does the pile of clothing surrender Joseph's sock.

Dhami, Narinder. *A Medal For Malina*. London: Hamish Hamilton, 1990. IL: Ages 5-8.

Malina trains for sports day until her ambitions are thwarted by an aggressive competitor.

Dinan, Carolyn. *Good Monster*. London: Hamish Hamilton, 1992. IL: Ages 4-6.

Joe cannot sleep. He imagines that the shape on the wall is a monster. Then he sees two large hairy feet sticking out from under his bed and huge teeth glinting. His mother reassures him that there is not a monster.

Dinan, Carolyn. *The Lunch Box Monster*. Boston: Faber and Faber, 1983. IL: Ages 4-6.

A little boy thinks there is a green monster in his lunch box. The boy thinks the monster is responsible for scaring a teacher away, protecting him from a bully, and frightening people at a local museum. The monster is also supposedly the one who messes up the child's room; however, the boy finds he must take the blame and straighten up the room.

Dunn, Phoebe. *Feelings*. Mankato, MN: Creative Educational Society, 1971. IL: Age 7-12.

This text interprets and illustrates various emotions children feel.

Feder, Jane. *The Night-Light*. New York: The Dial Press, 1980. IL: Ages 4-6.

Kate, who is afraid of the dark, feels she needs a nightlight. Her mother lets her select a nightlight; however, Kate finds the light looks too scary at night. Kate tries other kinds of lights but finds that they do not work well. She finds that the street light outside her window and the moon and stars are the best night lights.

Fine, Anne. *Only A show*. London: Hamish Hamilton, 1990. IL: Ages 5-8.

Each member of the class must give a little five minute show and Ann cannot think of a thing to do. But her talent does eventually come through.

Geras, Adele. *Nina's Magic*. London: Hamish Hamilton, 1990. IL: Ages 5-8.

A magical adventure for Josie and Ben where the worlds of reality and dream are intertwined.

Goffstein, M. B. *Me And My Captain*. New York: Farrar, 1974. IL: Ages 2-6.

This book deals with separation through doll characters. A doll imagines her life with another doll, a sea captain. When he is on a voyage, she waits for his return. The story attempts to help children deal with separation from parents.

Gurd, Len. *Jason Brown–Frog*. London: Viking, 1989. IL: Ages 5-9.

Jason Brown is afraid of water. He hates his swimming lessons and his bully of a swimming teacher. When a frog offers him a wish, an extraordinary adventure begins. Through this adventure Jason overcomes his fear of water.

Hamilton, Morse. *Who's Afraid of The Dark?* New York: Avon Camelot, 1983. IL: Ages 4-6.

Kate cannot sleep so she gets her father to tell her a story. Each time he begins a story, Kate's doll interrupts by telling the father about her fear of wastebaskets, curtains, and noises outside the house. The father and Kate reassure the doll about her fears, and after a brief story from the father, Kate falls asleep.

Henkes, Kevin. *All Alone*. New York: Greenwillow, 1981. IL: Ages 4-8.

This story helps small children cope with separation. A number of positive aspects of separation are presented.

Henkes, Kevin. *Sheila Rae, The Brave*. Viking: London, 1988. IL: Ages 2-6.

All the bravado in the world fails to help her when Sheila Rae gets lost. Scaredy Cat Louise helps Sheila find her way.

Hill, Susan. *Pirate Poll*. London: Hamish Hamilton, 1992. IL: Ages 3-6.

Polly is afraid of people in masks and with painted faces. Her school decides to have a pirate day, Polly becomes very nervous. Her teacher finds a way to make the day less frightening and Polly discovers that dressing up is fun.

Jones, Rebecca. *The Biggest, Meanest, Ugliest Dog in The Whole Wide World*. New York: Macmillan, 1982. IL: Ages 2-6.

Jonathan is frightened of a huge dog that lives in his neighborhood. Each time the dog scares Jonathan he runs to his house, crosses the street, or climbs a tree. One day when Jonathan throws a ball at the dog, the dog returns the ball to Jonathan. This becomes a game and is the beginning of a friendship between Jonathan and the dog.

Julian-Ottie, Vanessa. *One Night At A Time*. London: Hamish Hamilton, 1989. IL: Ages 3-7.

A book that encourages children to believe that childhood fears can be overcome.

Kalb, Jonah, and Viscott, David. *What Every Kid Should Know*. Boston: Houghton Mifflin, 1976. IL: Ages 7-11.

This text presents problems of growing up and gives suggestions on coping with various emotions.

Kraus, Robert. *Whose Mouse Are You?* New York: Macmillan, 1970. IL: Ages 2-6.

A small mouse is separated from its parents. By the end of the story, all family members are back together.

Lindbergh, Reeve. *Midnight Farm*. London: Hamish Hamilton, 1987. IL: Ages 5-12.

An illustrated story that helps children deal with night-time fears. The book presents a summer night setting in the country.

Little, Jean. *Different Dragons*. London: Puffin, 1987. IL: Ages 8-12.

Ben makes a discovery which proves that he is not the only one who is afraid of a few things.

Little, Jean. *Jess Was The Brave One*. London: Hamish Hamilton, 1992. IL: Ages 5-8.

Jess is practical and not scared of anything. Claire is overly imaginative and scared of everything until the day Pink Ted is stolen. Claire proves that an active imagination can be more useful than plain common sense.

Livingston, Myra Cohn, and Sis, Peter. *Higgledy-Piggledy: Verses and Pictures*. New York: Macmillan, 1986. IL: Ages 6-8.

This text helps children vent frustrations over unrealistic expectations of them.

Marcus, Irene Wineman, and Marcus, Paul. *Scary Night Visitors*. New York: Magination Press, 1990. IL: Ages 3-8.

This book is for helping children understand and manage fear. A second theme of the book is that having very powerful feelings does not result in angry wishes coming true.

Mark, Jan. *Nothing To Be Afraid Of*. London: Puffin, 1982. IL: Ages 11-14.

A collection of unusual and startling short stories about children sympathetically and honestly observed.

McPhaill, David. *Andrew's First Flight*. London: Puffin, 1990. IL: Ages 2-6.

A picture book for children who are flying for the first time or who are nervous about flying.

Morrison, Carl V., and Nafus, Dorthy. *Can I Help How I Feel?* New York: Atheneum, 1976. IL: Ages 7-12.

This text uses case histories to illustrate the distressful emotions of young people.

Oram, Hiawyn. *Jenna and The Trouble-Maker*. New York: Holt, Rinehart & Winston, 1986. IL: Ages 5-7.

This book helps children deal with troubles by helping them understand where problems come from. The author uses a Yiddish folktale and artwork to deal with the topic.

Peck, Richard. *Through A Brief Darkness*. New York: Viking, 1973. IL: Ages 10-14.

Karen's father is an underworld figure. She tries to ignore the truth about her father. Her mother died when Karen was very young, and she is raised at a boarding school. In the story she is captured by a rival underworld gang of her father's. Karen is essentially alone at the end of the story, with no one to turn to.

Parenteau, Shirley. *I'll Bet You Thought I was Lost*. New York: Lothroop, Lee, and Shepard, 1981. IL: Ages 4-6.

Sandy becomes lost in a grocery store. He cannot find his family and resolves himself to living in the grocery store until his family's next shopping trip. Sandy runs into his father and pretends that nothing ever happened.

Preston, Edna Mitchell. *Where Did My Mother Go?* New York: Four Winds, 1978. IL: Ages 3-7.

The story is about a kitten who goes out searching for his mother. The theme of the book suggests ways children can deal with separation from parents.

Rodgers, Frank. *Who's Afraid of the Ghost Train*? London: Viking, 1990. IL: Ages 3-6.

Robert imagines all sorts of scary things. With some advice from Grandpa Jim he is not at all afraid of the ghost train, but his friends are.

Schubert, Ingrid, and Schubert, Dieter. *There's a Crocodile Under My Bed!* New York: McGraw-Hill, 1981. IL: Ages 4-6.

Peggy claims she can't sleep because of the alligator under her bed. The alligator, who happens to be friendly, delights Peggy with an evening of playing in the bathtub, dancing, and constructing an alligator model out of boxes. Her parents find the cardboard alligator the next day and think it explains Peggy's story, but she knows better.

Schwartz, Joel L. *Shrink*. New York: Dell/Yearling, 1986. IL: Ages 11-14.

A boy's parents take him to a psychiatrist because of poor grades. He finds that needing someone to talk to is not disgraceful, and it helps to deal with troubling emotions.

Sharmat, Marjorie. *Frizzy The Fearful*. New York: Holiday House, 1983. IL: Ages 4-6.

Frizzy Tiger is scared of almost everything and constantly makes up excuses to keep his friends unaware of his fears. Although he is terrified of leaving his house, Frizzy must venture out for food. He encounters a mud puddle, swinging doors, and a juicy lemon, all things that he fears. When Frizzy sees a friend in trouble, however, he must conquer his fear of climbing to rescue her and decides to face the mud puddle next.

Shaw, Diana. *Make The Most of A Good Thing: You!* Boston: Atlantic Monthly Press, 1986. IL: Ages 11-14.

The author covers the problems that preteen and teenage girls face. Included are the emotional and physical changes they must deal with.

Simon, Norma. *Why am I Different?* Niles, IL: Whitman, 1976. IL: Ages 7-11.

The story offers ways that children are different and attempts to help them deal with fears related to their differences.

Smith, Susan. *The Night Light*. Chicago: Follet Publishing Company, 1981. IL: Ages 2-6.

William the bug is not frightened by such things as spiders, the wind, or deep water; however, he is afraid of the dark. William temporarily solves the problem by capturing a lightning bug to use in his bedroom. The lightening bug wants his freedom, so he teaches William how to always have a night light, by closing his eyes and thinking about bright things.

Snell, Nigel. *Danny Is Afraid of The Dark*. London: Hamish Hamilton, 1982. IL: Ages 4-6.

Danny hurriedly prepares for bed, certain that there are monsters hiding in the dark in his bedroom. When Danny calls for help, his mother comes and reassures him that he only imagined the monsters. The monsters leave the room, sad that Danny doesn't believe in them anymore.

Stevenson, James. *We Can't Sleep*. New York: Greenwillow Books, 1982. IL: Ages 4-6.

Louie and Mary Ann, who are unable to sleep, are eager to hear a story from their grandfather. Grandpa describes a sleepless night he had as a child and what he did to get tired, such as swimming across the ocean, running 50 miles, and fighting a dragon. At the completion of Grandpa's story, which concludes with him safe at home, Mary Ann and Louie have fallen asleep.

Stren, Patti. *I'm Only Afraid of The Dark (At Night!!)*. Scarsdale, NY: Bradbury Press, 1985. IL: Ages 4-6.

Harold the owl lives with his family in the Arctic Circle. He is afraid of the night and even hates to close his eyes. Winter is approaching, bringing 24 hours of darkness a day. Harold and his friend work together to overcome their fear of darkness.

Sussman, Susan. *Hippo Thunder*. Niles, IL: Albert Whitman and Company, 1982. IL: Ages 4-6.

A family tries to help a child deal with his fear of thunder. The child is not reassured about his fear and heads for his parents' bedroom. The father teaches the child how to count between lightning and thunder to gauge how far away a storm is, and this helps the child deal with his fear.

Szillagyi, Mary. *THUNDERSTORM*. Scarsdale, NY: Bradbury Press, 1985. IL: Ages 2-6.

A little girl while playing in a sandbox looks up to see a thunderstorm approaching. She runs to the house, and her mother comforts the child. The small girl in turns comforts her trembling dog; after the storm both return to play.

Tomlinson, Jill. *The Owl Who Was Afraid Of The Dark*. London: Puffin, 1991. IL: Ages: 4-6.

A baby barn owl named Plop is afraid of the dark. Human and animal friends help him face his fear and overcome it.

Weiss, Nicki. *Waiting*. New York: Greenwillow, 1981. IL: Ages 2-7.

A child is left at a gate while her mother goes off shopping. When the mother returns, the child is very happy. Even though a responsible parent would never leave a child in such a predicament, children will recognize the fear of abandonment and will find examples of how to deal with this fear.

Zolotow, Charlotte. *The Summer Night*. New York: Harper, 1974. IL: Ages 4-8.

When a small girl's mother is away, she is cared for by her father. The story deals with how fathers can care for children when mothers are away.

Abingdon Press
P.O. Box 801
201 8th Avenue
Nashville, TN 37202

Adama Books
306 W. 38th Street
New York, NY 10018

Addison-Wesley Publishing
  Company
1 Jacob Way
Reading, MA 01867

Aladdin Books
866 3rd Avenue
New York, NY 10022

Annick Press
Ragged Appleshaw
Andover, Hants., SP11 9HX
United Kingdom

Arlington Books
P. O. 327
Arlington, VA 22210

Atheneum Publishers
866 3rd Avenue
New York, NY 10022

Atlantic Monthly Press
19 Union Square West
New York, NY 10003

Avon Books
1350 Avenue of the
  Americas
New York, NY 10019

Bantam Books
666 5th Avenue
New York, NY 10103

Barron's Educational Service
P. O. Box 8040
250 Wireless Blvd.
Hauppauge, NY 11788

Beacon Press
25 Beacon Street
Boston, MA 02108

Berkley Books
200 Madison Avenue
New York, NY 10016

A. C. Black
35 Bedford Row
London WC1R 4JH
United Kingdom

Blackie
Wester Cleddens Road
Bishopbriggs,
Glasgow G64 2NZ
United Kingdom

Bradbury Press
866 3rd Avenue
New York, NY 10022

Carolrhoda Books
241 1st Avenue North
Minneapolis, MN 55401

Child Welfare League of
  America
440 First Street, NW
Washington, DC 20001

Child's World
224 West Van Buren Street
Chicago, IL 60607

Children's Press
5440 North Cumberland
  Avenue
Chicago, IL 60656

Clarion Books
215 Park Avenue South
New York, NY 10003

Collins
15 Oakenbrow
Sway, Lymington
Hants., 5041 6DY
United Kingdom

Comp-Care Publications
2415 Annapolis
Minneapolis, MN 55441

Coward-McCann
Incorporated
200 Madison Avenue
New York, NY 10016

Creative Education
Incorporated
123 South Broad Street
Mankato, MN 56001

Thomas Y. Crowell Company
10 East 53rd Street
New York, NY 10022

Crown Publishers
Incorporated
201 East 50th Street
New York, NY 10022

Delacorte Press
666 5th Avenue
New York, NY 10103

Dell Publishing Company
666 5th Avenue
New York, NY 10103

Dembner Books
61 Fourth Avenue
New York, NY 10011

Andre Deutsch
106 Great Russell Street
London WC1B 3LJ
United Kingdom

Dial Books
375 Hudson Street
New York, NY 10014

Dillon Press
242 Portland Avenue
Minneapolis, MN 55415

Dodd, Mead & Company
  Incorporated
6 Ram Ridge Road
Spring Valley, NY 10977

Doubleday
666 5th Avenue
New York, NY 10103

E. P. Dutton
375 Hudson Street
New York, NY 10014

Eyre and Spottiswoode
8 Roe Green
Worsely, Manchester M18
4RF
United Kingdom

Faber
3 Queen Square
London WC1N 3AU

Farrar, Straus & Giroux
  Incorporated
19 Union Square West
New York, NY 10003

Follet Publishing
1000 West Washington Blvd.
Chicago, IL 60607

Four Winds Press
866 3rd Avenue
New York, NY 10003

Greenwillow Press
1350 Avenue of the
  Americas
New York, NY 10019

Hale
Clerkenwell House
45-47 Clerkenwell Green
London, EC1R OHT
United Kingdom

Hamish Hamilton
27 Wright's Lane
London W8 5TZ
United Kingdom

Harcourt Brace Jovanovich
  Publishers
1250 6th Avenue
San Diego, CA 92101

Harper Collins Publishers
10 East 53rd Street
New York, NY 10022

William Heinemann, Ltd.
Michelin House
81 Fulham Road
London SW3 6RB
United Kingdom

Holiday House Incorporated
425 Madison Avenue
New York, NY 10017

Holt, Rinehart & Winston
301 Commerce Street
Suite 3700
Fort Worth, TX 76102

Human Sciences Press
233 Spring Street
New York, NY 10013

Hurst and Blackett
38 King Street
London WC2E 8JT
United Kingdom

Alfred A. Knopf Incorporated
225 Park Avenue
New York, NY 10003

Lerner Publishers
241 1st Avenue
Minneapolis, MN 55401

Lippincott
10 East 53rd Street
New York, NY 10022

Little, Brown & Company
  Incorporated
34 Beacon Street
Boston, MA 02108

Little, Simon
1230 Avenue of the
  Americas
New York, NY 10020

Lollipop Power
P. O. Box 277
Carrboro, NC 27510

Lothrop, Lee & Shepard
Books
1350 Avenue of the
Americas
New York, NY 10019

Macmillan Publishing
Company
866 3rd Avenue
New York, NY 10022

Magination Press
19 Union Square
New York, NY 10003

McGraw-Hill Books
1221 Avenue of the Americas
New York, NY 10020

Julian Messner
Route 9W
Englewood Cliffs, NJ 07632

Morning Glory
6595 San Haroldo Way
Buena Park, CA 90620

William Morrow & Company
  Incorporated
1350 Avenue of the Americas
New York, NY 10019

Thomas Nelson Publishers
Nelson Place at Elm Hill Pike
Nashville, TN 37214

Norton
On the Green
Guilford, CT 06437

Orchard Books
387 Park Avenue South
New York, NY 10016

Pantheon Books
201 East 50th Street
New York, NY 10022

Parents Magazine Press
685 3rd Avenue
New York, NY 10017

Perspective Press
629 Deming Place
Chicago, IL 60614

Philomel Books
200 Madison Avenue
New York, NY 10016

Plus
27 Wright's Lane
London W8 5TZ
United Kingdom

Prentice-Hall Incorporated
Route 9 West
Englewood Cliffs, NJ 07632

Puffin Books
27 Wright's Lane
London W8 5TZ
United Kingdom

G. P. Putnam's Sons
2000 Madison Avenue
New York, NY 10016

Random House Incorporated
201 East 50th Street
New York, NY 10022

Rosen
658 Main Street
Placerville, CA 95607

Scholastic Incorporated
730 Broadway
New York, NY 10003

Science House
55th Avenue
Elmhurst, NY 11373

Charles Scribner's Sons
866 3rd Avenue
New York, NY 10022

Seabury Press
10 East 53rd Street
New York, NY 10022

Souvenir
43 Great Russell Street
London WC1B 3PA
United Kingdom

Lyle Stuart
600 Madison Avenue
New York, NY 10022

Ticknor & Fields
215 Park Avenue South
New York, NY 10003

Viking
375 Hudson Street
New York, NY 10014

Viking Kestrel
375 Hudson Street
New York, NY 10014

Walker & Company
720 East 50th Street
New York, NY 10019

Frederick Warne & Company
  Ltd.
27 Wright's Lane
London W8 5TZ
United Kingdom

Franklin Watts, Incorporated
387 Park Avenue
New York, NY 10016

Western Publishing
850 Third Avenue
New York, NY 10022

Westminster Press
100 Witherspoon Street
Louisville, KY 40202

Albert Whitman & Company
5747 West Howard Street
Niles, IL 60648

Woods Hole Historical
  Collection
P. O. 185
Woods Hole, MA 02543